# *COWBOY CUISINE:*
# *BEYOND BISCUITS & BEANS*

*Deanna Dickinson McCall and Gay Gardella*

Visit our website at www.whitebirdpublications.com

Hardcover ISBN: 978-1-63363-493-0
eBook ISBN: 978-1-63363-494-7
LCCN: 2020948733

We dedicate this book to our families and friends who have shared our tables through the years. We thank you for your encouragement in more ways than words can say.

Gay and I assembled this cookbook to share the culture of ranch cooking. We hope it appeals to everyone, from someone in New York City to the ranch cook in the middle of nowhere, from the accomplished chef to the beginning cook. Cowboy cuisine or cooking has come a long way from what most folks perceived as bacon, beef, beans, and biscuits. Chefs like Grady Spears and others brought the western table to levels equal to that of fine American and European dining. Like the ranches and cattle people from which the dishes come, it is honest, natural, and real food.

I grew up on old-time traditional ranch fare, but also had a granddad that cooked and ventured beyond those confines, as well as parents who knew and enjoyed great food. We all have special memories of favorite foods, and I hope you will want to create that for someone.

So-called "ranch cooking" varies widely according to regions, and often includes many ethnic dishes. I will say that ranch or cowboy cooking is best described as "food cooked on a ranch." I don't believe it needs to be put in the alley and sorted more than that.

You will find recipes that had their beginnings from Italian, Basque, other European countries as well as Mexican, and Great Britain roots, just like the folks on the ranches. I've even included an Oriental recipe or two. We tried to include everything from the simplest fare to dishes for special occasions.

In keeping with the long-needed return to real foods, you will find very little processed or artificial ingredients called for in this collection. I use real meat, real milk, real fats, and real sugars.

I learned to cook for one simple reason; I wanted great food. We had tight budgets and towns with restaurants were a long way off. I lived and raised a family without electricity for a couple of decades. We had propane refrigerators, a root cellar, and propane and wood stoves to cook on. My kids rolled gallon jars of cream across the kitchen floor to make butter. We picked and canned wild and domestic fruit or made jellies, and even canned an entire deer once. Watercress was picked from the spring for salads. I made bread every other day and there were always cookies, cakes, puddings, and pies for dessert. I also worked outside alongside my husband every day, riding and working cattle, and growing hay. Wish I had that kind of energy now. I still work on the ranch and ride a lot, but don't have the energy of that younger woman and mother, and no longer have seven or more people to feed three meals a day, every day.

I now live on a ranch that may seem remote to some, but, is pretty up-town to us. We have electricity, phone, and internet. This means having real fridges and freezers, modern appliances, and closer neighbors and friends that share the love of good cooking and great company. We often get together and try new recipes for our dinners. Or we share old favorites. In addition, I am an author of western-themed books and poetry and am a performing poet. We often have fellow writers and performers staying with us who love to share our table. That's what cooking is all about, sharing the product you've created out of love and caring, whether it is for a branding crew, family meals, guests, or a holiday.

You will find a wide range of recipes and ideas in this collection. Everything from simple, to more complex, and some very basic recipes that you can tailor to your tastes and preferences. I would like to encourage you to step outside that box or corral and try something new. Don't be afraid to experiment, to try new flavors and techniques. I will always remember the first time that I made a loaf of bread and the amazing feeling of accomplishment I experienced, to know I mixed those ingredients and the end product was this wonderful golden loaf that smelled so good. The satisfaction of creating something is immeasurable.

I encourage you to use the freshest, best ingredients you can find, and to even consider growing those products if you are able. I don't need to remind you there is no substitute for a homegrown tomato. Even the city dweller can now grow many things in pots, everything from herbs to peppers and tomatoes. If this isn't possible, that's all right, just buy the best ingredients you can.

I hope you enjoy this book and view it as a short visit to our table and lifestyle. We have a place set for you.

—Deanna McCall

Deanna McCall and I were destined to write a cookbook together, after all, our first meeting was over a great home barbequed steak dinner. As the friendship grew, we recognized we had many common interests and common passions: family, food, cows, horses, clear mountain air, and empty wine bottles are a few of them. It's a match made in Heaven! I guess I should throw cowboys in there, too, since we each have one that we love as much as life itself. John Lynch and Dave McCall are our biggest supporters and partners in life and crime. They are also our chief food critics. You'll get to know them as you read this book. Many of the dishes are their "fare with flair"!

Deanna and I share other common backgrounds. I came to live in New Mexico via California but was born in Nevada. I'm a true native "Desert Rat", as Nevadans are called. That doesn't sound very complimentary, but to true Nevadans it's endearing. Go figure! Though I've been gone for a long time, Nevada and its rugged western culture still means home to me.

Deanna came to New Mexico via Nevada but was born in California. We both lived our Nevada lives in the northern part of the state, from Reno in the west to Elko and the beautiful Ruby Valley country in the east. Ranches and sheep camps and the people that lived and worked them were the background for our lessons in the ways of the Great Basin west. That common history further formed the foundation for our friendship.

To make it all more interesting, we have our differences, too. After all, if two people are exactly the same, one of them isn't necessary. Right? So, it goes that we celebrate our different strengths and personalities. An award-winning author of western novels and poetry, Deanna regularly performs at Cowboy Poetry Gatherings around the country. I write lectures for college courses and read textbooks in my spare time. An Animal Science professor for many years, I specialized in Beef Production. It's what I love, what I know, what I do. Though retired from full-time teaching, I continue to teach online each semester for Bakersfield College in California. It's an amazing world we live in today where a non-tech cattlewoman can teach online from another state. Again, go figure!

When we cook, our creative sides come together. It is that creativity and the "joy" of cooking and serving good food that we want to share with you. Whether you're cooking for two or cooking for a crew, serving good food can be fun, easy, and very rewarding. Food brings people together; good food makes them look forward to being together. In the fast-paced world we all live in today, (yes, even cowboys' lives are faster paced than they used to be) the dinner table might be our last chance to hang on to some tradition, to family connections and bonds. Don't underestimate the power of time spent with family and friends sitting down to eat together.

Recently I read this poignant statement, "Time can't be saved; it can only be spent". The unstated admonishment is for us to spend it wisely. We think the time you spend with the two of you or a crew of you…family and friends around a dinner table…is time well spent.

In this cookbook-labor-of-love, our goal is to share with and encourage you to look at the opportunity to cook and share some good food with those you love. Like our kitchens, we hope your kitchen is now or will become, the hub of coming together to eat, talk, bond, and build memories.

Learning to be a great cook isn't hard it just takes a little imagination and practice. No one was ever born knowing how to be a Michelin Star chef, but just like any other skill, everyone can learn to be a good cook. Some will be better than others, but anyone can serve up delicious, memorable meals that keep their family and friends singing their praises and coming back for more. The recipes and stories in this book are designed to inspire you, simplify your time in the kitchen, and make you a star.

Whether you live in the city, the suburbs, or the wide-open spaces, we hope you'll ride along as we share the recipes that keep our friends and family coming home. Let's saddle up, cowboy up, and get cookin'!

—Gay Gardella

# TABLE OF CONTENTS

# *RISE AND SHINE BREAKFASTS*

## *PROTEIN BREAKFAST MUFFINS*

When all the kids were home on the ranch and we had a long day ahead of us riding, I made various things they could put in their pockets or saddlebags for snacks. Most of them were high in carbs, things like pocket sandwich turnovers, pancakes rolled with peanut butter, even the old syrup buckets (biscuits with a cavity made by sticking your thumb into it and filled with syrup or honey). We no longer need the high carbs, and I love to make these high protein "muffins". I prefer to grab one out of the fridge and eat it cold or wrap it and put in my pocket for when I'm riding and home is miles away. These are great for anyone on the go, kids to adults.

This is a basic recipe so you can add what you like. Vegetables like spinach, kale, or green chilis, or jalapenos are all good additions. For instance, Swiss cheese, ham, and spinach make a great combination, as does sausage, cheddar, and green chili. Just use your favorite ingredients to make what flavors make you happy. You'll feel better knowing you are eating right.

—Dea

## *Ingredients* (one dozen)

About 1 pound cooked breakfast meat, such as crumbled sausage or chopped ham or crumbled bacon
12 eggs (For the recipe use one egg and about 1 Tablespoon of cooked meat for each muffin cup.)
Seasonings such as garlic powder, black pepper, paprika, red pepper, etc.
Spinach, diced chile peppers, etc.
Grated cheese

## *Directions*

Preheat oven to 350 degrees
I suggest using a silicone muffin pan or greasing a muffin pan with solid fat, not liquid or spray.
Place about 1 Tablespoon of cooked meat such as sausage, ham, bacon, or even ground beef in greased tin.
Sprinkle desired cheese over meat, about 1 Tablespoon of cheese.
In a bowl, whisk the eggs. Use one egg per muffin cup. Add seasonings, such as garlic powder, black pepper, red pepper flakes, and a dash of tabasco. Add spinach, chilis, peppers, etc. if desired. Pour eggs over the cheese and meat 'til cup is about ⅔ full.
Bake 15 to 20 minutes, until a toothpick comes out clean when the muffin is tested.
Eat warm or store in fridge for a grab and go snack.

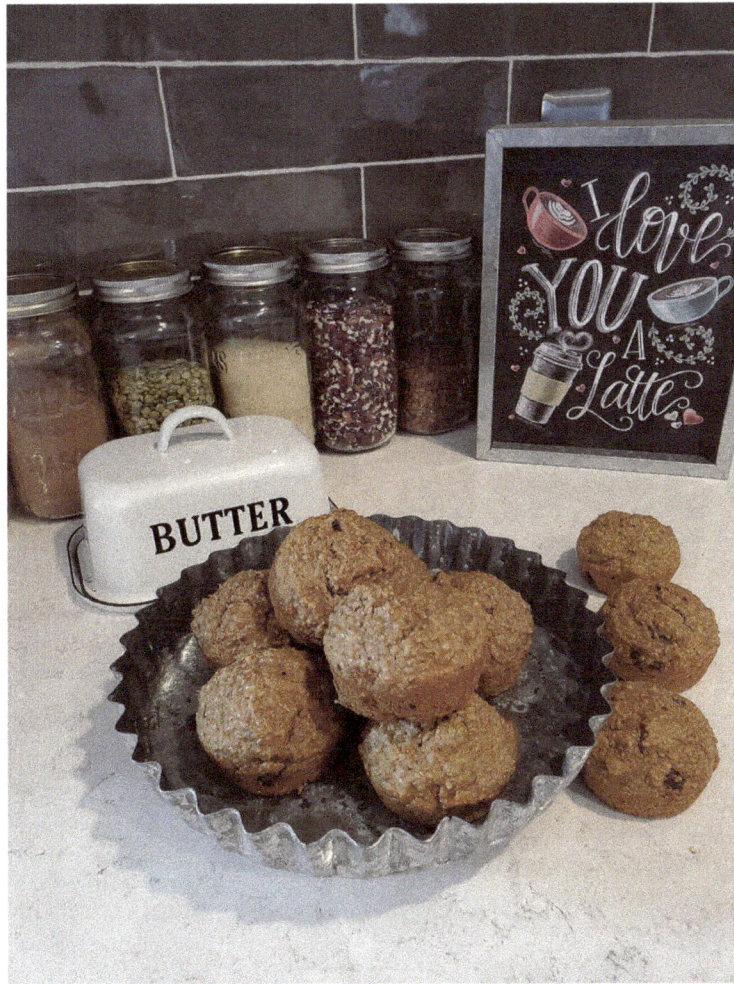

## BRAN MUFFINS EXTRAORDINAIRE

Bran Muffins are great for breakfast, but these are so decadent they could disguise as a dessert. Made with real bran instead of processed bran cereal, they're healthier, too. This recipe is actually one-fifth of the original recipe I got many years ago. It would make enough muffins to feed a logging camp, but you probably just need to feed a gathering crew of cowboys or a houseful of hungry H.S. athletes. Either way, these muffins will do the trick. They keep well and freeze, too, so make a batch for yourself to have for that quick on-the-run breakfast in the morning or a mid-morning snack at the office.

—Gay G.

## *Ingredients*

3 eggs
1 cup vegetable oil
3 cups buttermilk
1 teaspoon vanilla
¾ cup brown sugar
¾ cup molasses
2 cups honey (or try substituting 1½ cups maple syrup)
¾ cup dark raisins
¾ cup chopped walnuts
6 cups bran
5½ cups whole wheat flour
1 teaspoon baking soda

## *Directions*

Whisk eggs then add oil, buttermilk, vanilla, and brown sugar, and mix all together well. Add honey, molasses, raisins, and nuts. Mix well and set aside. In a larger bowl, mix bran, flour, and baking soda. Slowly add the liquid ingredients into the dry mix until well incorporated. Pour into paper-lined muffin cups and fill halfway. Big muffin cups work best, but regular size just makes a smaller muffin and more of them. Bake in preheated oven at 375 degrees for 12-15 minutes, or until test done.

*\*Note:* always adjust time and temperature for altitude above 4000ft.
Serve with butter because "Butter makes everything better", said Julia Childs It wasn't Julia's "first rodeo".

# *CHRISTMAS MORNING CASSEROLE*

This is probably one of the best breakfast casseroles I've ever had. It works well for any holiday breakfast or brunch, luscious and decadent. I've also served it on Easter and other special days. I especially love that you make it the night before, allowing you to visit with friends and family while it bakes. When you want to make something really special, this will do it. The use of croissants rather than bread, and the great cheeses in it make a memorable dish. Serve fresh fruit along with it and you have a great meal.

—Dea

## *Ingredients*

1 pound of good, hot breakfast sausage
1 cup of shredded Parmesan cheese
1 teaspoon salt
Black pepper
3 green onions
1½ Tablespoon of chopped chives
¾ pound of bakery croissants torn into small pieces
2 cups of heavy cream
2 cups of milk
6 eggs lightly beaten
1 cup of sharp Cheddar or Asiago, grated
1 cup of Gruyere cheese, grated

## *Directions*

Grease a 13 x 9 inch baking dish
Cook the sausage until done and well crumbled in a large pan or Dutch oven
Add the Parmesan, salt, a sprinkle of black pepper, onions, chives, and the torn-up croissants
Toss several times to mix, and then evenly spread into greased baking dish
Top with the Gruyere and Cheddar or Asiago
In a medium-size bowl whisk the eggs, add the milk and cream, gently pour over the ingredients
Wrap the dish in plastic wrap and refrigerate overnight or at least 8 hours
Preheat oven to 350 degrees
Uncover the dish and bake about 45 minutes, until golden brown
Let stand a few minutes before serving, then enjoy

## BREAKFAST ROUND-UP BAKE

Casserole doesn't have to be a "dirty" word these days. Baked dishes can be elegant combinations of textures and flavors that please even the most sophisticated palates, like cowboys. What I like most about casseroles is their versatility. Use them as great make-ahead side dishes or the main course. Serve them for breakfast, brunch, lunch, or dinner. This recipe for Breakfast Round-up Bake is easy to put together. It can be made ahead and kept in the refrigerator overnight. It bakes up to a flavor-packed nutritious crowd pleaser. Try it soon, it's sure to "rope 'em in"!

To make the eating experience more fun, purchase some of the pretty bakeware that is available for very reasonable prices today. After all, we eat with our eyes first, plus it's inspiring and motivating for the cooks (that's us) to present a pretty dish as well as one that's pleasing to the palate. I recently bought a beautiful red casserole baking dish at a local discount store. It takes casseroles to a new level. Your guests will be so impressed with the beautiful presentation and wonderful taste of your creation that the word "casserole" won't even enter their minds. Remember this golden rule: It only takes a little extra effort to make something ordinary into something extraordinary. Go for it!

—Gay G.

## Ingredients

1 large package frozen hash brown potatoes
1 package Jimmy Dean regular sausage
1 red bell pepper chopped
½ med yellow onion chopped
¾ cup fresh baby portabella mushrooms chopped
2 cups fresh baby spinach coarsely chopped
2 cups each of grated Cheddar cheese and Monterey Jack cheese
¼ cup butter
¼ cup olive oil
2 teaspoon each of salt, pepper, garlic powder

## Directions

Microwave hash browns a minute or so just to thaw enough to break them up. Put in large mixing bowl. Sauté bell pepper, onion, and mushrooms in olive oil and butter until just starting to become tender (about 3 minutes). Add spinach and sauté until cooked down (1-2 minutes). Pour veggies and all the oil into the hash browns and mix thoroughly. Cook sausage in same pan until done and crumbled. Add to hash brown mixture and combine thoroughly. Add cheeses, salt, pepper, and garlic powder. Mix well.

This mixture can be made a day ahead and sealed in a plastic container. Refrigerate until ready to cook then put in greased 9 X 13 casserole dish or in a large cast-iron skillet (our preference to get better-browned edges). Don't press the mixture down tightly; it will cook down. Bake in preheated 350 degrees oven approximately 35-45 minutes. When done it will be brown around the edges, cheeses will be visibly melted, and center will be hot to the touch. For crispier top, put pan under the broiler until desired brown is achieved.

Serve with fried or poached eggs on top or on side, sour cream, avocado slices, and salsa. Our standby red salsa is great, but be creative, try the green salsa, hot, medium, or mild.

Serves 6 generously

Variations: try red or green onions or a combination, use Hot or Sage sausage. Chorizo or Italian sausage can be substituted for regular sausage, too. The sky's the limit on this one so go for it! Just be sure to write your recipe down; you may find yourself getting requests.

## *OMELET BREAKFAST BAGS*

When you've got a crowd to feed this can make things much easier and is a fun alternative to standing over the stove like a short-order cook. This can be done indoors, or outdoors on the porch or patio or even while camping. You will just need to figure about ¼ cup of each ingredient and 2 eggs per person. Leftovers are great for this, such as cooked broccoli, spinach, or summer squash, and various meats. Just use your imagination.

—Dea

### *Ingredients*

Quart freezer bags
Eggs
Diced ham
Cooked crumbled sausages
Small pieces of cooked beef from steaks or roasts
Crumbled bacon
Cooked diced or grated potatoes
Diced green onions
Grated cheeses
Salt and pepper

Add-ons after cooking
Salsa
Avocado
Chopped chives or green onions
Toast or biscuits can be prepared and available if desired.

### *Directions*

Fill a large pot with water and begin heating it. It needs to reach a rolling boil. Meanwhile, prepare the ingredients above, placing each ingredient in a container with a spoon. You will place all the ingredients in a line, starting with the bags and ending with the large pot of boiling water. The procedure for your guests is to grab a bag, break 2 eggs into the bag, gently squeeze the eggs to break them a little, and then add whatever ingredients they want in their omelet. The bag is then pressed to remove some air, sealed, squeezed to mix the fillings, and dropped into the boiling water. Depending upon the size of the pot, several bags can be cooked at once. In two or three minutes, use tongs or a large slotted spoon to remove the bag when the eggs are cooked to satisfaction. The omelet may be eaten directly from the bag or emptied onto a plate. This is a great way to feed a bunch of people, and it's fun for kids to do.

## *COW CAMP BUTTERMILK PANCAKES*

This is a good opportunity to say a few words about buttermilk. You can judge by the space allotted to buttermilk in the grocery store that it is not a big seller. That's too bad because buttermilk is an amazing ingredient that can be used to add flavor to many recipes that don't even call for it.

Originally, buttermilk was a by-product of the process of making butter. After the butterfat was removed by the churning process, the leftover "whey" would be allowed to ferment creating a thick, tangy liquid known as buttermilk. Today the product we buy is produced by the addition of a bacteria culture to whole or reduced-fat milk, causing the fermentation process that results in the tangy flavor. Science lesson #1—

Bacteria is not a bad word. There are more beneficial bacteria than there are pathogenic bacteria (disease causing) and many of them are helpful, even necessary, for good health. Don't recoil when you hear the word bacteria, it doesn't mean we're talking about germs.

One of the problems with buying buttermilk is that we often only use a small amount of it and then the rest ends up sitting on the refrigerator shelf until it's outdated. Then we pour it down the drain. Pity. There are so many ways to use up the leftover buttermilk; you just need to be creative. It's much more than just the base for wonderful homemade Ranch Dressing! Have we said, "Be fearless in the kitchen!" before? Well, try thinking out of the box. Get out of the comfort zone. Buttermilk isn't just for biscuits and pancakes. Try it in any cake, cookie, or cream pie recipe as a substitute for regular milk. Use it in frosting…wow does it sharpen up the sugary taste! It can be substituted for milk or water in sauces and gravy. Don't waste it, make something that can use it. How do Buttermilk Pie, Buttermilk Pancakes, Buttermilk Waffles, and Buttermilk Jalapeno Cornbread sound? Meanwhile, try these easy Buttermilk Pancakes.

—Gay G.

## Ingredients

1¼ cups flour
½ teaspoon salt
½ teaspoon baking soda
2 teaspoon baking powder
1 Tablespoon sugar
1 egg
2 Tablespoon vegetable oil or melted butter
2 Tablespoon water
2 cups buttermilk (approximately)

## Directions

Combine dry ingredients. Beat egg, oil, and water with a fork to mix well. Add to dry ingredients along with enough buttermilk to make a good consistency batter—not too thick, not too thin. Add water or regular milk if you used all the buttermilk and need to thin it more.

Cook pancakes on a nonstick greased griddle or frying pan.

Delicious served with butter and syrups, jams or jellies, honey, or powdered sugar. Try strawberries and whipped cream for a special weekend breakfast or brunch.

## *BEST-EVER CINNAMON ROLLS*

I've made a lot of cinnamon rolls over the years and after coming up with this recipe I will never use another. The dough itself is so tender and light, and the filling wonderful and rich. This recipe works well at any elevation, and can be refrigerated for a few days in a plastic wrap covered bowl 'til ready to roll out and bake. Sometimes, I will bake one pan of rolls and then bake the other half of the dough a couple of days later.

—Dea

### *Ingredients for rolls*

2 cups of milk
½ cup oil
½ cup sugar
1 package yeast or 2½ teaspoon

3 cups of flour
1 ½ cups flour
½ teaspoon baking powder
½ teaspoon baking soda
½ Tablespoon salt
½ cup butter (1 stick) melted
½ cup brown sugar
2 to 3 teaspoon cinnamon
½ cup chopped nuts or raisins if desired

## Ingredients for icing

¼ cup butter (½ stick)
½ bag powdered sugar (1 pound)
2 teaspoon real maple syrup, use maple flavoring if you don't have real syrup
¼ cup whole milk or half and half
2 Tablespoon brewed coffee or 1 teaspoon coffee flavoring
Dash of salt

## Directions for rolls

Place in a saucepan the milk, oil, and sugar; heat until warm, but do not boil. Pour the heated liquid into a large bowl, let cool 'til just warm, and then add the yeast. Let sit a few minutes 'til some bubbles form. Add the 3 cups of flour, just until mixed. Cover and let rest for 1 hour.
In a small bowl mix 1½ cups flour, baking powder, baking soda, and salt. Add this to the dough and mix thoroughly, kneading a tiny bit if necessary. Cover and chill dough for 30 minutes or overnight.

Divide dough in half, covering the half you aren't using. Roll out on a floured surface into a rectangle; you'll want this thin, as the thinner the dough is the more filling the rolls will have. Pour or brush on about ½ cup of butter. Sprinkle on brown sugar, cinnamon, and nuts or raisins, if using. Beginning with the edge furthest from, you begin to tightly make a roll, rolling toward you. When you've completed the roll, place the seam on the surface, and gently rock it back and forth to seal. Using a sharp thin knife make slices about 1 to ½ inches thick.
Place 2 Tablespoon melted butter in a 9 x 13-inch pan and then place slices in pan. Do not crowd the slices. You will end up with 10 to 12 slices per pan, depending on the thickness of your roll.
Repeat the above procedure and cover both pans with a cloth to rest for around 20 to 30 minutes.
Turn the oven to 375 degrees. Once the oven is hot, bake the rolls 20 to 25 minutes, just until barely golden in places. You don't want a brown crust on these rolls. While the rolls bake, make the icing. The

icing will go on the rolls as soon as you pull them from the oven.

## Directions for Icing

In a bowl mix the butter, powdered sugar, maple syrup or maple flavoring, milk or half and half, brewed coffee or coffee flavoring, and a dash of salt. Whisk and stir this until it is well mixed, adjust the coffee and maple flavoring. Icing should be fairly thick. Spoon and spread the icing over the rolls as soon as they come out of the oven. The rolls will absorb a lot of the icing, filling the cracks and spaces of the rolls.

Yield: 20 to 24 rolls

## *COWBOY BREAKFAST PIE*

If you try to feed quiche to our cowboys, you'll get a lot of wincing and groaning, even though they're quite sophisticated gourmets. John and Dave know good food, but there's something disconcerting about the word "Quiche". It just doesn't sound manly enough. It conjures up images of ladies' light brunches with teas and chiffon pies. Not many respectable guys are going to admit to loving quiche no matter how modern they may be. After all, "Real Men Don't Eat Quiche," as author Bruce Feinstein's tongue-in-cheek book taught the world back in 1982, thus the reason we named this recipe Cowboy Breakfast Pie.

Quiche, frittatas, and omelets; is there a difference? Well, technically they are the same, but different. Start with eggs and milk and you have scrambled eggs. Add an unlimited assortment of meats, vegetables, cheese, and spices; cook it in a pan, then fold it over and you have an omelet. Now take the same ingredients, put them in a baking dish to bake and you have a frittata (with Parmesan cheese on top, of course. Very Italian). Or, take the same eggs and ingredients; put them in a piecrust; bake it in the oven; and voila! you have Quiche. See, they are the same, but different! So, I'm pretty sure cowboys like quiche if it's called a pie.

The really great thing about making quiche is the unlimited possibilities it presents to the cook. Generally, you'll need eggs and a combination of some meat, cheese(s), vegetables, and herbs/spices. Meet those requirements and your imagination is the limit. Try using cooked diced ham, crumbled bacon, chorizo, or breakfast sausage. One of the best ways to add some zip and zing is to try some unique cheeses. Cheddar, Swiss, and Monterrey Jack make excellent quiche and omelets, but why not be fearless and experiment with some of the other cheeses like Pepper Jack, Gruyere, Manchego, Smoked Gouda, etc., etc., etc. As for vegetables any onion, leek, or shallot will work, but you'll get the most flavor if you stay away from yellow or white onions. I prefer using the red or green varieties. Peppers are always good: yellow, red, green of any variety will add texture, color, and flavor. If you'll choose and use fresh peppers, you'll find the flavors will pop more than canned or frozen. Fresh broccoli, spinach, baby kale, zucchini, yellow squash, and tomatoes are my favorite veggies to add, but you can experiment. (Yes, everyone knows tomatoes are fruit!) Just remember, whatever you use needs to be compatible with the meat and cheese variety you choose. Here's a tried and true Quiche recipe that almost everyone will love. If you're new to quiche baking, start with this recipe and then experiment from there. Have fun!

—Gay G.

## *EASY PASTRY*

### *Ingredients*

4 ounces cream Cheese
½ cup butter
1 cup flour
¼ teaspoon salt

Combine softened cream cheese and butter. Mix until well blended. Add flour and salt and mix well. Form into a ball, cover with plastic wrap and chill for 1 hour (or make the day before). On lightly floured surface, roll out to an 11-inch circle. Place in a 9-inch pie pan. Trim and flute the edges; prick sides and bottom with a fork to reduce shrink. Bake at 450 degrees for 12-15 minutes. Use a pie ring or aluminum foil around the edge to prevent over browning. Remove when done and set aside to cool while you make filling. Note: you don't have to bake before filling the crust, but it will be a flakier crust if you do. Also, I sometimes make it in a springform pan. It makes a beautiful pie and the crust is strong enough for it to stand alone on a serving plate.

## *COWBOY BREAKFAST PIE FILLING*
(aka CANADIAN SWISS QUICHE)

### *Ingredients*

7 eggs
2 Tablespoon butter
¼ cup milk
2 teaspoon flour
½ cup diced Canadian bacon
3 thinly sliced green onions, shallots, or leaks
1 cup chopped fresh spinach
¾ cup diced or shredded swiss cheese
8 halved grape tomatoes
¾ teaspoon salt
½ teaspoon black pepper

### *Directions*

In a skillet, melt butter on medium-low heat. Add Canadian bacon, onions, spinach, salt, and pepper. Sauté stirring gently until onions start to soften and spinach is cooked down. Set aside. In a mixing bowl, combine eggs, milk, and flour. Whisk or beat until smooth and there are no flour lumps. Add vegetable mix to eggs, and then stir in cheese. Pour egg mixture into cooled pastry; place pie ring or foil on top to prevent edge from burning, and bake at 350 degrees until knife comes out clean when inserted in the center (about 30 minutes, but watch and check as it cooks). The top may start to brown. If edge needs more browning, remove ring the last few minutes. Garnish with grape tomato halves. Serve with a side of fruit (optional).

Serves 5-6 regular people or 2-3 hungry cowboys.

# *SAUSAGE STRATA*

This is an easy, delicious breakfast casserole that is perfect when accompanied with a cup of fruit or some sliced melon. Growing up, my kids called it breakfast pizza. The recipe is easy enough that kids can make it with a bit of supervision. This is also great for a quick easy dinner when served with a crisp green salad. Prepare the fruit or greens while the strata bakes.

You may use any type of bread, from white sandwich, hearty grain, or even French bread. A family favorite is to use Cheddar cheese, but any combination of cheeses will work. I've also replaced the sausage with diced cooked ham for a change of pacc.

—Dea

## *Ingredients*

1 pound breakfast sausage, cooked, crumbled, and drained or diced cooked ham
6 or more slices of bread
1 cup of grated cheeses
4 eggs slightly beaten
1 cup of milk
1 cup of cream
1 teaspoon of Worcestershire sauce
Salt and pepper

## *Directions*

Grease a 13 x 9-inch pan and lay the sliced bread in the pan to cover the bottom. Spoon the cooked sausage evenly over the bread and then sprinkle the grated cheese over the sausage.

In a bowl, lightly mix the eggs, then add the milk and cream, Worcestershire sauce, and salt and pepper until well blended. Pour over the layers.

Bake at 325 degrees for around 30 minutes or until set. Let stand 5 or more minutes before cutting squares and serving.

## *CHERRY CHEESE DANISH*

Who doesn't love going into a local bakery and seeing those pastries behind the glass? This recipe makes just as pretty a pastry as you'll find almost anywhere and it is fast and easy. Any pie type filling can be used and the cream cheese is optional. If I am in a hurry, I grab a can of pie filling. If it is fresh fruit season, I make the filling. While this recipe is titled Cherry Cheese Danish; apple, blackberry, blueberry, peach, etc. fillings work well, also. Puff pastry comes with 2 sheets in a box; this recipe will use both sheets.

—Dea

## *Ingredients*

1 can of pie filling or 1½ cup of fruit cooked with ½ cup water, ¼ cup sugar, 2 teaspoon cornstarch, and 1 teaspoon cinnamon 'til it resembles canned pie filling
1 package of cream cheese cubed
1 box of puff pastry, thawed
Slivered almonds
Decorator or colored sugar optional

## *Directions:*

Preheat oven to 375 degrees
Thaw pastry sheets, place on parchment paper, and gently roll out a bit into a nice rectangle
Place half the filling down the center of each sheet
Dot with cubes of the cream cheese, using half the brick for each sheet
Beginning at the top corner of the sheet make a cut diagonally just short of the filling, you will be making cuts about an inch wide, repeat, and do the other side
Fold up the ends on each end of the pastry
Now, lay the first strip over the pastry; lay the next one from the opposite side over it. You are making a braid of sorts, keep laying the strips, alternating from side to side. Don't worry if the filling is oozing, or if your braid isn't exact, it will puff and be beautiful.

Bake at 375 degrees for about 30 minutes, 'til golden brown

You may also glaze the Danish with a mixture of powdered sugar, heavy cream, and flavoring, or sprinkle with slivered almonds and decorator sugar if desired

# *HUEVOS RANCHEROS*

There are many versions of this classic dish, translated as Ranch Eggs. Some varieties will have beans, some may have a meat chile, but all will be based on corn tortillas, eggs, and a spicy red or green sauce. This is one of the versions, a very basic version that's quick to prepare, sometimes served with a flour tortilla or fried potatoes or a side of pinto beans.

I've included my Basic Chile Gravy recipe. I use this sauce on everything from enchiladas to steak. It is the old, ranch ready staple using chile powder rather than the dried chiles.

—Dea

## *Ingredients*

Corn tortillas
Fresh Eggs
Chile Gravy
Grated cheese

## *Directions*

Quickly heat the corn tortillas in a little oil, cook just until the tortilla is softened, drain on paper towels, and cover to keep warm.
Have Basic Chile Gravy (recipe follows) warm
Fry eggs to desired doneness

To assemble, place 2 warm corn tortillas on a plate, overlapping slightly. Pour Chile Gravy over tortillas, sprinkle generously with grated cheese, and top with 2 eggs. Offer salsa to add on top of the eggs. A layer of either refried or pinto beans may also be added, as well as chile con carne if a heavier dish is desired. A modern addition is to add fresh avocado or guacamole.

## *BASIC CHILE GRAVY*

My grandad was born and grew up in Texas; he spent considerable time in Arizona, and then lived in California. His family came from Alabama before going to Texas. His cooking had a very definite southern to southwest flair. I probably inherited my love for cooking and for food from him. This is one of the recipes he always made and we used it for lots of things, from pouring it on eggs and meats to using it for enchiladas. The flavor and heat will vary depending on the type of chile powder you use. We rarely buy any red enchilada sauces since this is so much better and fresher, and only takes a few minutes to make. It also freezes well, so it is another recipe I will sometimes double.

—Dea

### *Ingredients*

¼ cup of oil
¼ cup of flour
2 to 4 Tablespoon of red chile powder
1 Tablespoon garlic powder
1 Tablespoon onion powder
2 teaspoon cumin powder
1 teaspoon Mexican oregano
1 teaspoon black pepper
2 cups of chicken broth

### *Directions*

Pour oil into a pan (you will use equal amounts of oil and flour)
Once the oil is hot, add the flour, whisking it in 'til you have a brown roux
Then add and stir in:
chile powder to taste and garlic powder, onion powder, cumin, Mexican oregano, and black pepper, stir in chicken broth
Keep whisking 'til smooth and let simmer for at least 20 to 30 minutes. Taste, add salt if necessary, and cook until it has reached the desired thickness
For a change of pace, you can try adding one or a combination of some of the following:
1 teaspoon of cinnamon along with 1 Tablespoon of tomato paste
Sliced or chopped jalapenos
½ teaspoon red pepper flakes
1 teaspoon smoked paprika

Juice of 1 lime

# *NEW MEXICO STYLE EGGS BENEDICT*

I used a variation of Gay's green chile gravy recipe to make this dish. It is a New Mexican version of Eggs Benedict, using a rich green chile cream gravy in place of the Hollandaise sauce. Either Canadian bacon or a slice of ham can be used, both work great with that green chile flavor. You can also add some creamy jack cheese if you like. While original Eggs Benedict calls for poached eggs, any soft-cooked egg will work. You will need that nice runny yolk to mix with the sauce.

—Dea

## *Ingredients*

4 English muffins
8 eggs
8 slices of ham or Canadian bacon
1 cup heavy cream
2 cups of whole milk
3 Tablespoon flour
2 Tablespoon butter
½ teaspoon of chicken base or bullion
1 can of chopped green chiles or the equivalent of fresh or frozen roasted green chiles
Salt and pepper
Paprika
½ cup grated Monterey Jack cheese (optional)

## *Directions*

Lightly fry/sauté the ham in the butter, drain, and set aside to keep warm. Stir the flour into the leftover butter until all the flour is absorbed, add more butter if needed to get all the flour incorporated into the butter. Then whisk in the milk, cream, green chiles, and chicken base. Cook and stir 'til thickened to desired consistency, adding more milk if needed. Fold in the cheese, if using. Cream gravy thickens as it cools. Adjust salt and pepper, and cover to keep warm. Poach or soft cook the eggs while the muffins are toasting.

Place 1 split toasted buttered muffin on each plate, then place a slice of the meat on each muffin, topped by an egg. Check the gravy for consistency and add a bit of milk if necessary. Spoon some of the gravy over the egg, and sprinkle with a bit of paprika before serving.

# *STARTING OUT RIGHT APPETIZERS*

# *EASY CHEESE SPREADS AND DIPS*

We enjoy a great variety of cheese and it seems I always end up with some odd pieces that I used to throw into cheese sauces. I discovered something else to do with them, and that is to make some outstanding cheese spreads or dips. Don't be afraid to mix cheeses, but do make sure you have some harder ones, like cheddar. Because you will always use different varieties and different amounts of them this will never come out the same, but will always be delicious. I roast and dice a sweet red pepper for this. You can also use chopped, roasted green chiles, from the can, freezer, or fresh for a different flavor. Or some jalapenos or other peppers. The use of mayo and cream cheese and butter will dictate the consistency. Just remember that those spreads using butter and cream cheese will need to be taken out of the fridge a little beforehand or they will be too stiff to spread easily. Hand grating the cheeses will provide a rougher texture; the use of a food processor will make a smoother spread.

Grate leftover cheeses either by hand or cube and place them in the food processor, you'll want to have about a cup after grating. If you have lots of cheeses, you can double the recipe. These recipes are far better than any kind of smoked gouda or pimento spread you will find on a store shelf, and much more economical. As always, don't be afraid to experiment with flavors.

—Dea

## *BASIC CHEESE SPREAD*

### *Ingredients*

½ cup mayo and ½ cup cream cheese
2 teaspoon red wine vinegar
1 teaspoon Worcestershire sauce
1 teaspoon liquid smoke flavoring
1 teaspoon granulated garlic
Cooked crumbled bacon, optional
1 to 2 cups of grated cheeses
2 Tablespoon chopped roasted red sweet pepper

### *Directions*

Place all ingredients together in a food processor if you want a smooth texture. Otherwise, place all ingredients in a bowl. Add black pepper and adjust salt, many of the ingredients contain salt, so taste before adding! Mix well.

Place in a plastic or glass container with a tight lid or use plastic wrap to cover and allow flavors to mellow.

Serve with veggies or crackers; you can even use this on a burger for a new delicious taste twist.

## FRENCH STYLE CHEESE SPREAD (FROMAGE FORT)

### Ingredients

About 1 pound various cheeses, cubed
½ stick of room temperature butter
1 teaspoon minced garlic
¼ cup of dry, white wine
2 Tablespoon chopped chives
Fresh ground black pepper

### Directions

Whir/pulse cheeses in food processor. Add the rest of the ingredients and pulse until mixed. You may adjust consistency by adding a bit of mayo if it is too thick or stiff. You may serve now or place covered in the fridge. This will need to come up to room temperature to be spreadable. It is wonderful spread on baguettes and broiled, and is also good just spread on thin crusty slices of bread or crackers.
This will keep in the fridge for a week, and it will become stronger and more intensely flavored as it sits and ages. Fromage Fort is translated as "strong or fortified cheese."

## *SKINNY DIP'N*

Serve this dip with sticks of carrots, green and red pepper, celery, zucchini, etc. and it qualifies for a Keto dip. It's also good with chips or pita bread, but you won't be qualifying for the "skinny" brigade if you eat too much of it. Really, eating dip is comfort food and it's not supposed to be for perpetual dieting so we'll call it SKINNY DIP'N and you can take the plunge off the high-dive later. You'll still feel better about eating it than if we called it Hefty Dip; right? See how we think?

Use this recipe as a base for other dips. Add chopped clams or crab meat for a delicious seafood dip.

—Gay G.

### *Ingredients*

⅔ cup mayonnaise
1 cup sour cream
1 Tablespoon fresh chopped parsley
2 green onions chopped fine, include some tops. You want about 2 Tablespoon of onion
1 teaspoon dried dill (because fresh dill is hard to find, but it's better of course. Use 1½ teaspoon fresh)
1 teaspoon garlic powder
1 teaspoon salt

### *Directions*

Mix all ingredients together and chill several hours before serving. If you prefer some heat, just add a few drops of Tabasco or other brand of hot pepper sauce.

# *SAVORY CHEESECAKE*

I never really thought about cheesecake being anything but sweet until I saw a recipe for savory cheesecake. Yes, there are a lot of dip and appetizer recipes that call for cream cheese, but a savory cheesecake, with a crust? So, I began experimenting and came up with this basic recipe. I will often change the cheeses and the crust ingredients and haven't had one that wasn't great. This is another recipe where you can utilize those last bits of wonderful flavored cheeses in, too. Swiss, Gruyere, Blue, Cheddars, Parm, etc., are all great. The same holds true for the crust, you can use any mixture of crumbs you like, from a variety of crackers to panko, and about half of the crumbs called for can be replaced with finely chopped nuts. You can even add some Parm or Asiago to the crust, if you really want to kick up the flavor. I often add minced garlic and sometimes other seasonings, depending on the cheeses you use. This is something different to put out with your usual appetizers. It can be enjoyed on crackers or toasted baguette slices, or on sliced veggies, or just by itself. Once again, don't be afraid to experiment; just think of the flavors you love. You can mix this by hand, but either an electric or stand mixer sure makes it easier.

—Dea

## *Ingredients*

1 cup fine crumbs
5 – 6 Tablespoon melted butter
2 packages cream cheese (16 ounces total)
½ cup of sour cream
1¼ cup assorted cheeses
2 eggs
Desired seasonings
Other possible ingredients such as crumbled bacon, finely diced ham

## *Directions*

Preheat oven to 375 degrees. Coat a 9-inch spring form or pie plate with cooking spray.
Mix crumbs with melted butter in a bowl, if it doesn't want to stick together add another Tablespoon butter.

Press firmly into pan, going partially up the sides, too. Bake for 6 to 10 minutes, just until set, and then set aside to cool while making the filling.

Reduce oven to 325 degrees

In a mixer bowl beat cream cheese 'til fluffy, beat in sour cream and eggs 'til smooth. Add in the cheeses and the seasonings, such as onion powder, cayenne, Italian blends. Stir in anything else you might want to add like cooked crumbled bacon or ham, finely chopped peppers such as jalapenos, red roasted peppers, or green chiles. Pour into the crust and bake 45 to 60 minutes until the top is lightly browned and the center barcly set. Leave the cheesecake in the oven with heat off and door cracked for an hour, then place on cooling rack. This can be served warm from the oven, room temperature, or chilled. Refrigerate leftovers.

## *COWBOY CAVIAR*

Cowboy Caviar is a classic relish/dip to serve for any occasion. You don't really need a crowd; it's fine and fair to serve it all for yourself. There are literally dozens of Cowboy Caviar recipes floating around. You can also buy it in some specialty stores, but this recipe is easy to make and a classic Texas-style version. Don't be afraid to add your own twist to it. Some suggestions are listed at the end. Serve with crackers or corn tortilla style chips. Use the "scoop" kind so you can fill 'em up. A cold beer goes great with Cowboy Caviar. Saddle up and enjoy.

—Gay G.

### *Ingredients*

1 15-ounce can Black-eyed Peas, rinsed well and drained
1 15-ounce can Black Beans, rinsed well and drained
1 11-12 ounce can sweet corn (not creamed), drained
1 cup finely diced red onion
½ cup finely diced green bell pepper
½ cup finely diced red bell pepper
12-15 grape tomatoes cut into 4 pieces each
1 cup coarsely chopped fresh cilantro (parsley can be substituted for all or some)
½ cup vegetable or olive oil
⅓ cup red wine vinegar
3-4 Tablespoon sugar
1 teaspoon red chili powder
1 teaspoon salt
½ teaspoon garlic powder

### *Directions*

In large bowl, mix together all of the beans and vegetables, except cilantro. In small bowl, make dressing by whisking oil, vinegar, sugar (to taste, less if you don't want it as sweet), chili powder, salt, and garlic powder.

Pour over bean-veggie mix and stir well. Add cilantro and lightly mix again. Cover and chill until ready to serve (at least 2 hours for better flavor). Give light toss just before serving. Serve with corn or tortilla chips or crackers.

*Options:*
Try adding chopped avocado just before serving.
Use canned Purple-hull Peas instead of Black-eyed Peas.
For a bit more zip, add one seeded and chopped Jalapeno pepper.

# *QUINCE AND MEMBRILLO*

When we moved to this old ranch there was a remnant of an old orchard and struggling fruit trees scattered around. We saved the trees that we could and discovered three of the trees were called quince. The only quince I was familiar with is an old-fashioned spring-flowering shrub. I was puzzled by the large, yellowish-green fruit that somewhat resembled pears, were as hard as an apple, but had fuzz like a peach. When I cut one open, there was the star seed formation common to apples and pears. I quickly discovered they were woody, bitter, and not pleasant. I tried leaving them on the tree to see if they would ripen, and as weeks passed the fruit never changed, but their fragrance became wonderful, making my entire yard smell like a vanilla/citrus/floral candle. My quince trees bear tons of fruit, regardless of late frosts, and other issues. So, I had to learn to utilize this odd fruit and began researching and visiting with folks about it. After all, someone loved them enough to plant several of them, I had to figure out why. I learned quite a bit about quince from an elderly ranch woman who had lived on our place, and other local ladies. One story about the origins of quince is that it is a predecessor of the apple and pear, and it is reputed to be the fruit that Eve gave Adam in the garden.

Research showed me the fruit is still highly prized in places like Spain, Italy, France, and Mexico. Quince paste or Dulce de Membrillo is available in limited quality at certain specialty stores, as are the actual quince fruits. Membrillo is the name of the quince fruit in Spanish language-based countries. I learned it must be cooked to be edible and it is very high in pectin, the stuff that makes jelly set. While the quince fruit is a whiteish color inside similar to the apple and pear, cooking it makes it become a lovely ruby color. The longer you cook it, the deeper the color.

The local ladies used it like pears in making a heavy syrup called Quince honey, to be used in place of maple syrup or bee honey. They also made jelly. I eventually found recipes for using it in lamb stew, in pies and tarts, and for making the famed membrillo that is so delicious when served with a slice of Manchego cheese. Manchego cheese is a Spanish cheese from the milk of Manchego sheep. Asiago or any aged cheese also works.

I experimented for a few years making membrillo, jellies, and even quince sauce. Quince sauce is like apple sauce on steroids, so good! And so easy, just cook the quartered, unpeeled quince in enough water to cover until very soft. Smash the pieces and press through a sieve or strainer or run it in your food processor and then strain to remove seeds. Add a bit of sugar and cinnamon, along with a dash of lemon juice and it is wonderful!

If you'd like to make a more conventional jelly (not as firm as the membrillo) just follow the recipe for apple jelly included with pectin boxes.

To me, there is a big difference between quince jelly and real membrillo. The jelly doesn't have the drier texture of the "dulce" or "candy" membrillo. Membrillo takes a long time to make but is so unique. I make it and gift it to special folks during the holidays. If you get it dry enough, it is also great cut into small pieces and rolled in sugar for a true fruit candy.

—Dea

## MEMBRILLO or QUINCE PASTE

### Ingredients

8 peeled and cored quinces cut into cubes
White sugar
2 Tablespoon lemon juice
1 teaspoon vanilla extract
Water

### Directions

Measure the amount of chopped, prepared quince and place in large, heavy pot like a Dutch oven.
Add ¾ to 1 cup of sugar for every cup of quince
Add lemon juice and enough water to cover the quince.

Cook on low heat, stirring occasionally to prevent sticking, this will take several hours. Use a potato masher to break down the quince once the pieces begin to soften. Cook until very thick, add the vanilla, and then puree the mixture by placing it in a food processor or using a hand blender.
Pour into a parchment paper-lined pan.

You can leave on the counter or place in the refrigerator to cool and set up. If the membrillo isn't as firm as you like you have a couple of options. One is to place the pan into a very low oven, 125 degrees for an hour or two. Another is to simply place it up in a cupboard for a few days like they do in Europe. Once set to your preferred consistency, wrap it in wax paper and store in the refrigerator or freeze. I make mine in the Fall and just store it in the refrigerator until around Christmas when I begin to serve it and give it away for gifts. It will also very gradually dry in the fridge.

# *SAVVY SOUPS AND SALADS*

# *MINESTRONE SOUP*

This is a meatless soup, other than the beef broth, but it won't offend even the most die-hard carnivore. Rich, thick, and hearty, it will fill up the hungriest crew. Serve it with salad, lots of crusty French bread, butter, and plenty of extra Parmesan cheese to put on top. If you also include an Antipasto plate with some salami, cheese, and pepperoncini, no one will even notice the absence of meat in the soup.

There are many versions of Minestrone Soup because, like many Italian dishes, it's a way to use the extras or leftovers in the refrigerator. You can really have fun experimenting when making soups and this one is no exception. After a while, you'll have a good feel for what does (and sometimes doesn't) go together. If you're still a bit timid about making your own soup version, start with this one. Remember, like all soups, it will be better the second day after the flavors have had a night to hang out together so go ahead and make it the day before if you're so inclined.

—Gay G.

## *Ingredients*

1 cup dry white beans
10 cups water
2 cans beef broth
1 can stewed tomatoes
2 stalks chopped celery
1 large or 2 medium zucchini
½ head of medium size cabbage diced (or I often prefer to use a whole medium head of Napa cabbage)
½ bunch of fresh spinach, washed and coarsely chopped
1 small yellow or white onion chopped
¼ teaspoon dry sage
½ Tablespoon Italian seasoning
¼ teaspoon red pepper
¼ teaspoon black pepper
1½ teaspoon salt
¾ teaspoon ground thyme
Dry spaghetti

## *Directions*

Rinse dry beans and sort out any blemished ones. Cover with water and soak overnight. This is an optional step, some people think beans must be soaked, but they really don't. Drain off water, combine white beans and 10 cups fresh water, and simmer on low heat with a lid on until the beans begin to get soft. Add the rest of the ingredients, except the spaghetti, and simmer on low for 1 hour. Bring soup to a soft boil and add one small handful of spaghetti broken into 2-inch pieces. Cook until pasta is done. Check seasoning and add salt accordingly to taste.

Crockpot method: Combine all ingredients in crockpot, except spaghetti, and cook on low until beans are soft (about 5 hours). Add spaghetti, turn to high, and cook until pasta is done. If you're not ready to eat the soup then, turn it back to low until serving time or turn off, cool, and refrigerate until the next day.

Serves 6

# *GREEN CHILE CHOWDER*

Nothing warms you like a cup of velvety soup on a cool day and this is a favorite for early Fall. I always keep bacon ends on hand for seasoning and it adds wonderful flavor to complement the corn and green chile flavors. This is a fairly quick and easy soup to make, using ingredients many of us have on hand. I often replace store-bought stock with bullion or paste and the correct amount of water. Canned, evaporated milk can also be used to replace the cream. Any variety of summer squash can be used. We keep roasted green chile both in the freezer and canned on the shelf for many dishes.

—Dea

## *Ingredients*

1 cup diced bacon ends
⅓ cup diced celery
1 finely diced carrot
½ of an onion
¾ cup of grated or diced zucchini
2 teaspoon minced garlic
3 cups of corn (fresh or frozen)
½ cup of chopped roasted green chile
2 cups of chicken stock
1 can of kidney beans, drained
1 cup of milk
1 cup of cream
1 cup of grated cheese; Cheddar, Jack, Asiago, any combination of them is good

## *Directions*

In a Dutch oven sauté the onion, celery, carrot 'til it is soft, and bacon has rendered some fat. Add the zucchini, garlic, corn, green chile, and cook for a few minutes until zucchini is soft.
Then add chicken stock, and kidney beans, simmer for 5 minutes before adding milk, cream, and cheese. Simmer at very low heat 'til heated through and desired thickness is reached.

Adjust seasoning, being careful not to over-salt as some ingredients contain salt. Serve with cilantro as a garnish, if desired

## SAUSAGE VEGETABLE SOUP

Here's a soup recipe that I threw together one day. I was stuck in the house, recouping from a bad cold, and knew Dave would welcome a warm bowl of soup when he came in. He does like good food, and soup is something he usually welcomes. I'm lucky in that he has never been a picky eater or afraid to try something new.

As I've mentioned, I try to keep a wide range of frozen and canned ingredients on hand, so I can just throw things together to make a dish when I need to. Homemade soups are always so warm and comforting, and they may make eating those tasteless, over-processed, canned soups a thing of the past. Serve a nice piece of crusty bread with this and a fresh, bright salad for a great meal.

—Dea

Ingredients

½ cup chopped bacon ends
2 small-med or hot Italian sausages removed from their casings, or ½ pound of bulk breakfast sausage
¼ cup olive oil
½ cup chopped celery
½ cup chopped carrots
½ onion diced
3 teaspoon minced garlic
4 or 5 small sweet peppers
1 cup chopped frozen or fresh broccoli
¾ to 1 cup of frozen or fresh chopped spinach
1 can diced Italian style tomatoes
4 cups of water
2 teaspoon chicken base
Heavy cream
Black pepper
Red pepper flakes
¼ cup of shredded Parmesan (optional)

## *Directions*

Place a Dutch oven over med heat. Pour in the olive oil, add the bacon ends, sausage, celery, carrot, and onion. Sauté, stirring occasionally, breaking up sausage as it cooks. When sausage is cooked and onion soft, add in the garlic, cook for a minute more. Add the peppers, broccoli, spinach, and the tomatoes, mix well and allow to cook 2 to 3 minutes. Pour in water; add the chicken base and black pepper, and red pepper flakes. Allow to simmer over low heat for 45 minutes to an hour. Add the cream, milk, and cheese; continue heating; don't allow to boil. Top with cheese, if desired.

*Note:* You probably won't need to add any salt; be sure and taste first.

## *BASQUE SOUP*

Deanna and I have had the privilege of knowing a lot of Basque people. They are a unique culture, a people without a country. The Basque originate from the Pyrenees Mountains that form a border between Spain and France. They have their own language, which is very different from either French or Spanish, and a wonderful culture. The Basque community is very close, and they continue to teach their children about their history, dances, and foods. As a culture, they cling to their values of family, work, and community.

Many of the Basques immigrated to the U.S. as sheepherders and you will find lamb on the menu in their homes and in all their restaurants. Across the western states of the Great Basin and into California, there are many young people who are following the tradition of their Basque fathers and grandfathers and continue to ranch. Some of the most successful cattle and sheep operations are still in the original families that immigrated from their Basque homeland years ago.

If you ever have the opportunity, visit one of the Basque restaurants located in Idaho, Nevada, and California. Take a crew with you, as the family-style serving is always more food than you can eat. If you happen to clean up a plate, just ask for more. They will gladly bring you another heaping plate of food. Depending on whether the owners are Spanish or French Basque, the courses will vary, but soup is traditionally the first course followed by a green salad, pickled tongue, beans, French fries (theirs are to die for), a pasta, a vegetable, and a meat entrée, all served with great French bread. I'm hungry just writing about it! If you get a chance, do track down a Basque restaurant or try this easy fresh vegetable soup. For a variation, try adding some Basque Beans or cooked pinto beans. If you add a little red wine and some salsa to your bowl, you can close your eyes and feel like you're in the Pyrenees Mountains!

—Gay G.

### *Ingredients*

3 medium potatoes cubed
4 carrots chopped
1 chopped onion
3 cloves chopped garlic
½ small head of cabbage cut into 1-inch pieces
1 8-ounce can tomato sauce
2 Tablespoon olive oil
1 teaspoon thyme
2 teaspoon parsley (you know how we feel about parsley…fresh, always use fresh.)
Pinch of crushed red peppers
2 cartons beef broth (32 ounce size)

5 cups water

## *Directions*

In a large pot or Dutch oven, sauté potatoes, carrots, and onions in olive oil. When onions are soft, add all other ingredients. Cover, bring to a low boil, then turn down, and simmer for 1 hour or until ready to serve.

Serves 6 generously

# *SAUSAGE SOUP*

This soup is a meal in a bowl and a hit with all ages. Fall and winter just beg for soup. It is true comfort food at its best. There's something special about a hot bowl of soup with friends and family around the table. Don't hesitate to invite a crowd for a winter soup supper. Serve with a nice green salad and warm fresh bread of your choice, crusty French is always a winner. That's all you need, good soup and good company!

—Gay G.

Ingredients

1 package Jimmy Dean regular sausage
2 Tablespoon olive oil
1 cup cubed raw potatoes
3 cloves chopped garlic
1 chopped onion
1 diced green or red bell pepper
1 can (12 ounce) stewed tomatoes
2 cans (12 ounce) kidney beans (with juice in can)
2 cartons Beef Broth (32 ounce size)
2 cups water
½ teaspoon ground thyme
1 Tablespoon dried Italian seasoning or fresh herbs (basil, rosemary, and oregano)
½ teaspoon black pepper
1½ teaspoon salt

## *Directions*

Brown sausage in soup pot with olive oil. When meat is done, add all other ingredients; stir well. Cover and simmer on low for 1 hr. This works well in a crockpot, too. Don't worry about exact cooking time. The soup will just keep getting better. In fact, it can be made the day before and reheated when ready to serve.

Serves 6 generously

## *HEARTY RANCH SOUP*

This hearty soup comes from Italian and Basque roots. I keep many of the ingredients in the freezer, freezing cabbage works very well when it is to be used in a cooked form in recipes. The freezing breaks the cabbage down, making it soften in less time. The finer the cabbage is chopped the quicker it will break down and become soft. I always have bacon ends in the freezer; I can slice off what I need for seasoning, and I also keep a variety of frozen vegetables, either from the store or garden. This is a basic recipe; feel free to play with both the ingredients and seasonings. Pasta or rice may be added if desired. This makes a comforting winter meal when served with Sheepherders or French Bread.

—Dea

In a Dutch oven sauté the following in 2 Tablespoon olive oil:

1 chopped onion
½ cup bacon ends
½ to ⅓ head of chopped green cabbage
1 finely chopped carrot
1 rib of celery finely chopped

When the onion and cabbage become soft add:
3 cloves minced garlic
1 chopped sweet or bell pepper
1 cup of tomatoes, fresh, frozen, or canned

Cook a few minutes then add:
2 cups of beef stock or broth
2 cups of water
1 Tablespoon dried Italian seasoning
1 teaspoon dried sweet basil
Black pepper to taste
Pasta or rice if desired
Pinch of red pepper flakes

Cook for an hour or more, you can't really overcook this soup. Add additional water if needed. You can even use a crockpot at this point. Or continue cooking on your stovetop for another hour, if time allows. Finish by adding:

1 can drained kidney beans and allow beans to heat up. Add ¼ cup of dry Parmesan or Romano cheese. Cook for a few more minutes, adjust seasonings.
Serve piping hot and topped with more cheese, if desired.

# *RUSTIC CLAM CHOWDER*

The great thing about this soup is that it's done and ready to serve in about 45 minutes, including prep time. A lot of soups need to cook quite a while on simmer to get the flavor developed, but this soup is ready to go as soon as all the ingredients are cooked through. If your crew doesn't like clams (or at least they THINK they don't), you can leave them out. Then it becomes Cowboy Bacon 'n Potato Soup! That will get their attention. Enjoy this hearty, filling soup on cold wintery days. Try it in a thermos for a warm-up lunch on the go, at the office, in a school lunch box, or for a "stick-to-your-ribs" dinner at the end of a long, cold day fixing fence. It's Soup for the Soul, we say! You may want to double this recipe if serving it to a crowd.

Here's a tip to remember when using thickeners, like flour and cornstarch. Always use a new spoon each time you taste it or the enzymes in your mouth will break down the thickener. By the next day, your dish will be watery and thin, and you'll wonder what in the heck happened to it. Stick to the rule: one taste per spoon.

—Gay G.

## *Ingredients*

4 slices smoked bacon (2 if thick cut) chopped in small pieces. (Don't use a maple or sweet-flavored bacon.)
1 cup chopped white or yellow onion
2 Tablespoon flour
1 6.5 ounce can chopped or minced clams with juice
3 medium washed & diced russet potatoes (unpeeled = rustic style)
½ cup diced celery
2 cups whole milk
½ cup heavy cream or half and half. (How rich do you like it?)
2 Tablespoon butter
1 cup grated cheddar cheese
Salt and pepper to taste
Chopped green onions or parsley for garnish

## *Directions*

In large Dutch oven or soup pan, sauté bacon until done but not crisp. Remove from pan and drain on paper towel. Be sure to leave drippings in the pan. Add onion, celery, and sauté until slightly tender, stir in butter to melt then add flour and stir until flour is mixed well. (Note: If the bacon was too fatty, you may have too many drippings. Remove a Tablespoon or 2 if you think it's too much but reserve it and add back into flour mix if needed to be sure all the flour is well mixed with oil.)

Add potatoes and clams with the juice and cook over medium heat until potatoes are soft (about 15 minutes). Add milk, cream, and seasoning (salt and pepper) to taste. Cover and simmer for 20-30 minutes on low heat. Just before serving, add cheese and stir well to melt cheese. Dish into soup bowls and garnish to serve.

Serves 4

# *24-HOUR SALAD*

This is a clever salad because you can make it 24 hours ahead of serving time and still have a fresh, crisp salad to serve when you're ready. It's also pretty. The red cabbage adds flavor, texture, and great color! For a large group, you'll want to double or triple accordingly and you'll appreciate the fact that it's ready to serve when you're ready to eat, there won't be any last-minute fuss getting the salad put together so it will be fresh and crisp at serving time. If you've ever experienced a wilting salad when the rest of the meal is ready, you feel my pain. Fresh, crisp salad is one of my passions. You might say I'm a salad fanatic and have a hard time feeling like a dinner menu is complete without some version of a green salad. Wedge, Caesar, Mixed Spring Greens, Spinach, and any other type of fresh green salad can finish off a classic dinner menu. This 24-Hour version is a great salad choice when you're taking it on the road for a picnic, potluck, branding, family holiday dinner, etc., but it's just as great served at home, too.

—Gay G.

## *Ingredients*

½ head iceberg lettuce, shredded
½ head red cabbage, shredded
½ box or bag frozen peas (fresh if they're in season)
3 hardboiled eggs, chopped
⅓-pound bacon, diced and cooked
Mayonnaise
Seasonings (salt, pepper, seasoned salt)

## *Directions*

Layer first 6 ingredients in salad bowl
Top with generous layer of mayonnaise to cover and seal layers below. Cover and chill overnight or for 24 hours. Just before serving, toss layers to mix all ingredients, adding salt, pepper, and seasoning salt to taste. Add more mayonnaise if necessary. Serve with tomato garnish, if desired. Options
Add 3 Tablespoon of capers as you toss and reduce salt for an upscaled version.
Add 1½ Tablespoon Red Wine Vinegar when tossing salad.

Serves 6

## *COUNTRY TATER SALAD*

My husband reminded me this is my most requested recipe. So often potato salad can be disappointing, blah, too much mustard or not enough, perhaps needing salt and lacking flavor. This dish is always a favorite when I take it to a branding, covered-dish supper, or to a barbeque or picnic. Red potatoes or russets are my favorites for this recipe, and I don't peel either variety. The two big things to remember are that you are actually making a dressing, not just using mayo, and to salt the taters as you add them. Hope you enjoy this recipe as much as we do.

—Dea

### *Ingredients*

1¼ cup real mayonnaise (I use Best Foods)
2 Tablespoon apple cider vinegar
2 teaspoon prepared mustard
2 Tablespoon white sugar

1½ teaspoon table salt plus more for later
Good sprinkle of black pepper
5 hard-boiled eggs, chopped
½ cup chopped red onion
½ cup chopped dill pickle or dill relish
½ cup chopped celery
1 sweet red pepper diced
6 to 7 medium/large potatoes (about 5½ cups) boiled and cubed

## Directions

Boil potatoes 'til just tender. Allow the potatoes to drain and cool while making the dressing. Combine the first 6 ingredients in a large bowl, add everything except the potatoes, and mix well. Add 1 layer of potatoes to the dressing in the bowl and salt and pepper that layer, and then fold the potatoes into the dressing. Repeat with the remaining potatoes, salting and peppering each layer before folding into the bowl. Once all the potatoes are mixed in garnish by sprinkling with a bit of paprika and some dried parsley.

Store tightly covered in the fridge until ready to serve.

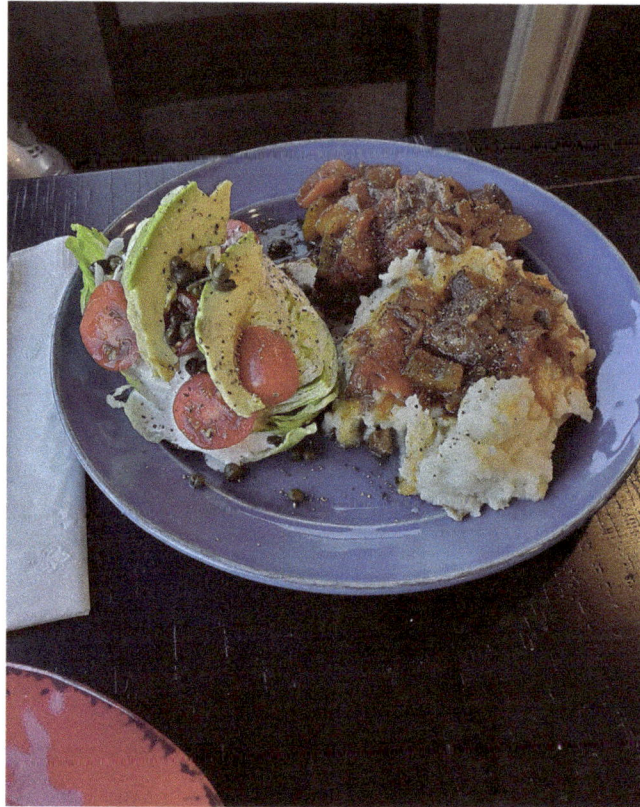

## PANHANDLE WEDGE SALAD

The Panhandle of Texas is one of the major cattle feeding regions of the United States. Hereford, Texas, located 48 miles south of Amarillo, calls itself "The Beef Capital of the World" and in true Texas-style, they're darn proud of it. It's the land that inspired old movies and stories about the big ranches and famous cattle drives from Texas north to Kansas and Montana. Charles Goodnight ranched there and signs for the XIT, Four Sixes, and others still exist. It's cattle country through and through.

Along with the millions of head of cattle, they also have wind in the Texas Panhandle. It blows and blows and blows. George Strait may have arrived by morning, but he failed to tell you about the wind. If the wind isn't blowing in Amarillo, it's considered a Chamber of Commerce Kind of Day. We spend a lot of time in the Panhandle every month because John has several large clients there. One day, when I first visited Amarillo, we were walking with a friend, at least trying to walk. I was in fear of blowing away and asked Dr. D. Hutcheson if the wind always blew that hard. He said, "Well, yes. You see, there's nothing between here and the North Pole but a barbed-wire fence, and it's down!" I've told that story so many times and get a hardy laugh every time. It exemplifies what I like about Texas, i.e. the Texans. They have great spirit, senses of humor, and are defined by western culture. It runs through their veins.

Another thing I like about Texans, Texas, and Amarillo is a local restaurant establishment named Macaroni Joe's. Set in a strip mall, first-timers are surprised by the ambiance when they walk into a Tuscan village, where tables appear to be set on a quaint Italian sidewalk. A fully stocked wine cellar is in view behind glass doors and one expects an upper story window, complete with Geranium filled flower boxes, to open and an Italian appear shouting down a greeting to the diners below. Wendy and the rest of the staff are always happy to see you and Chris, the Sommelier, is sure to have just the right wine to pair with your dinner and a new port to taste with your dessert. The service is impeccable, and the menu is as unique as the setting with appetizers like Flaming Mob Queso and entrees like Osso Bucco, Steak Diane, Seafood Cioppino, Maple Farms Duck Breast, and Pan Roasted Seabass.

Regardless of what I choose as my entrée, I always start with their Wedge Salad. Always! I'm a wedge salad fanatic and I've tried them all around the country. Macaroni Joe's is the best. In fact, I love it so much I finally took the time to develop my own version, which we're sharing with you. It's not a substitute for Macaroni Joe's, you still need to go for the atmosphere and all the other goodies they serve, but you can make this Panhandle Wedge and enjoy it at home as often as you'd like.

Amarillo is a dynamic community, it's one of the fastest-growing cities in the country and has a diverse economic base, but don't forget the cowboys and the cattle industry that built the town and is still a driving force today. As we've emphasized by the title of this book, cattlemen and cowboys aren't defined by a chuckwagon serving biscuits and beans anymore. Today they are educated, sophisticated professionals who enjoy good food with the best of them. One of the charms about dining at Macaroni Joe's is the fine dining Tuscan atmosphere dotted with patrons in Wranglers and cowboy boots. Like all cultured cowboys, they say, "Yes, Ma'am", and take their hats off at the dinner table. That's real Texas, and real Texans! That's worth a Wedge Salad any day!

—Gay G.

## Ingredients

1 medium head of iceberg lettuce
½ package prosciutto coarsely chopped
Grape or cherry tomatoes cut in half
Red onion sliced thin
Capers (drained)
Blue Cheese Dressing (see recipe)

Blue Cheese crumbles
Fresh ground black pepper

## *Directions*

Peel outer leaves off the Iceberg and cut in half and then into quarters. On each quarter, cut off the core, leaving just a little to hold the wedge piece together. Place on individual plates and then top with dressing, prosciutto, tomatoes, onions, capers, and crumbles, in that order. Finish with fresh ground pepper. The amount of each item depends on your own preferences. Serve immediately.

Serves 4

*Note:* If using a large head of Iceberg, you can cut into 5-6 pieces and get more servings out of it.

## *SALAD DRESSINGS*

The importance of good salad dressing is often overlooked. To be perfectly honest, there aren't any great dressings that come from the grocery store and the reason is they have to contain stabilizers in them and preservatives of some sort to keep them shelf safe for an extended period of time. These additives aren't necessarily unhealthy; they just don't add to good flavor. Salad dressings are so simple to make at home and much less expensive, it just doesn't make good cent$ to buy them. We've included some dressing recipes that are sure to please and will make your salads worth the time it takes to make them. If you're going to eat rabbit food, make it good rabbit food. By the way, cowboys eat rabbit food, too!

—Gay G.

# BLUE CHEESE SALAD DRESSING

## Ingredients

½ cup Best Food Mayonnaise (or Hellman's)
½ cup Sour cream
½ cup Buttermilk
½ cup crumbled blue cheese (use the best brand you can find)
1 Tablespoon Hidden Valley Ranch dry dressing mix
¼ teaspoon black pepper
1 clove fresh garlic

## Directions

Combine all ingredients into blender or bullet machine (best choice). Mix until all ingredients are well blended. Chill for at least 2 hours before tossing green salad. Top with some extra blue cheese crumbles. You can substitute Roquefort, Gorgonzola, or Cambozola cheese for a subtle taste variation. Adjust amount as needed to taste.

# CREAMY CAESAR SALAD DRESSING

## Ingredients

1 cup Best Food Mayonnaise (or Hellman's)
2 teaspoon Anchovy paste (more if you want, taste first)
1 large clove of smashed or chopped garlic
½ cup finely grated Parmesan cheese
3 – 4 Tablespoon lemon juice (preferably fresh)
Salt and pepper to taste (remember the anchovy paste is also salty)

## Directions

Combine all ingredients in a blender, food processor, or bullet machine (best choice). Process until well blended. Refrigerate for at least two hours before tossing over fresh Romaine lettuce. Top with croutons and shaved or shredded Parmesan cheese and fresh ground black pepper. Keeps well in the refrigerator. Note: this dressing's taste will develop as it chills for a while so don't get too zealous about altering the recipe until you've tried it as is. After it's chilled for an hour or so, taste test and adjust according to your taste. You may like more lemon flavor or more anchovy. That's usually all you'll need to adjust. Make it your own, make it your way. Remember, you can't really ruin it, if you find one flavor is overpowering the other, add some mayonnaise and you'll be back in business.

# *CLASSIC VINAIGRETTE SALAD DRESSING*

## *Ingredients*

½ cup light olive oil (use regular if light oil is not available)
½ cup red wine vinegar
1 teaspoon salt
¾ teaspoon black pepper (fresh ground preferably)
4 Tablespoon Dijon Mustard

## *Directions*

Blend all ingredients thoroughly. A blender, bullet mixer, or submersion mixer can be used if available and will blend the oil and vinegar better. Pour desired amount over salad and toss. A little extra fresh pepper added when you're tossing the salad will really add to the flavor of the salad.

Put extra dressing in covered container and refrigerate until ready to use. Bring to room temperature and shake well before using.

This recipe makes enough for 2 average size salads. You can double or triple the recipe to have plenty of dressing on hand. It keeps well for up to a month.

*Tip:* Use a glass jar with sealing lid or decorative jar to store the dressing (available at Walmart, Hobby Lobby, and other outlets). Because fresh homemade vinaigrettes all tend to separate, it's best to dress the salad before serving rather than putting dressing on the table for individuals to dress their own.

# MAIN EVENT DISHES

## *EASY ASIAN RIBS*

You may be surprised to find an Oriental recipe in a cowboy cookbook. Just remember Hoss, Little Joe and Ben on the Ponderosa had Hop Sing as their cook; even back in those times, ranchers and cowboys knew good food. I like this recipe as a different way to use beef ribs, particularly spareribs. Depending upon the cut of ribs you have, try to cut them into smaller pieces. The ribs cook all day in a crockpot so at supper time you can have the whole meal on the table in a few minutes.

The bright colors and exotic flavors make for a great change of pace. You can take the basic recipe here and serve it over rice, if you prefer. If you're watching calories, the stir-fried veggies are a healthier alternative. I like to serve it with a bowl of egg flower soup for a great meal.

—Dea

## *Ingredients*

½ cup soy sauce
½ cup brown sugar
1 Tablespoon sesame oil
1 Tablespoon chile oil
1 Tablespoon rice or wine vinegar
2 Tablespoon fresh minced ginger
4 cloves minced garlic
½ teaspoon of red pepper flakes
4 to 5 pounds of beef ribs

## *Directions*

Place everything except the ribs in a crockpot. Mix well. Add the ribs, turning them to coat with the sauce in the crockpot. Cook on high for 4 or 5 hours or all day on low.

Turn off crockpot, remove ribs, and strain fat from liquid. Pour sauce into a saucepan, return ribs to crockpot to remain warm. Add 1 cup of grated carrots, 1 small zucchini (cut in small pieces) into saucepan; bring to boil, and let simmer a couple of minutes.

To serve, place ribs on a serving of white cooked rice. Spoon sauce over, sprinkle with chopped green onion and sesame seed.

Or do the following while the sauce is simmering:
Heat 2 Tablespoon of oil in a large skillet, add 6 cups vegetables, and cook 'til tender/crisp
Add the ribs to the skillet, pour sauce over, stir, and lift 'til sauce is thickened
Place on serving plate and sprinkle with sesame seeds and chopped green onions

# *BARBACOA*

When I was a kid, some of the folks in California still made the old-style form of barbacoa, usually a bull's head buried in a pit with wonderful spices and cooked overnight. It worked well for brandings, meetings, weddings, and other events where hungry folks gathered. The head would be raised up after cooking at least a night and half a day, and the hide was peeled back to expose moist, perfectly cooked meat.

There are many variations of this dish, most with the same or similar spices used to make the unique spicy, sweet flavor. This is one of the versions I use, and a slow cooker ensures tender, flavorful results. I learned the home-style way to serve both barbacoa and pork verde in the manner I suggest below from some great Mexican cooks. Please don't be afraid to play with the spices, adjusting them to your personal taste.

—Dea

## *Ingredients*

4 pounds of beef, (stew meat, chuck roasts, whatever tougher boneless beef you have)
4 Tablespoon oil
4 Tablespoon flour
1 chopped onion
2 chipotle peppers in adobo
2 guajillo peppers, seeded and scraped
4 teaspoon minced garlic
1 Tablespoon ground cumin
1 Tablespoon oregano
1 teaspoon cinnamon
2 teaspoon beef paste or bullion
2 cups water
Juice of 1 lime
Black pepper

## *Directions*

Salt and then lightly flour the meat, then brown in the hot oil. Transfer the meat into the crockpot; add the rest of the ingredients.
Cover and cook all day (I don't think you can overcook this)
Remove the meat, and allow to rest, and then chop or pull with 2 forks. Return the meat into the broth, and mix well, taste to see if salt is needed. Sometimes, at this point, I put the meat along with all the sauce in

the fridge, then reheat, and serve it the next day

To serve, place a flour tortilla on a plate, spoon meat on half of the tortilla with slotted spoon, close the tortilla, and ladle sauce over the tortilla. Finish with a dollop of sour cream or yogurt if desired.

# *CORNED BEEF AND CABBAGE IN BEER*

Corned Beef and Cabbage is a traditional meal on St. Patrick's Day in America. Ironically, the Irish of Ireland don't share the tradition. Never the less, it's a great dish and worthy of inclusion in this book of recipes. Made from less expensive cuts of beef like a brisket, the meat is "corned" or cured in a salty, seasoned brine for at least seven days. Then it is slow-cooked to create a uniquely seasoned and tender cut of meat. To make life easier, buy it already brined and ready to cook to save some extra work and time. Cooking it in a crockpot makes it easy and allows the flavors to develop.

Plan to buy ¾ pound of meat for each person you will serve because it will cook down considerably. You'll want extra because those Corned Beef sandwiches the next day are too good to miss!

One year, along with my friends and neighbors, Kathy and Sylvia, we served Corned Beef and Cabbage at a Kern County Cattlewomen's meeting/luncheon that happened to fall on St. Patrick's Day. It was a big hit; we received so many compliments that day! If my memory is right, we had 6 crockpots going and I don't remember any leftovers!

A word of advice on buying your Corned Beef. There are basically two kinds, rather two cuts of brisket commonly used to make Corned Beef. You'll find either a point cut or a flat cut. You need to look at the meat carefully and buy the leanest one. Otherwise, you can end up with a little bit of corned meat and a lot of corned fat. I prefer to buy the point cut, sometimes called the melon cut Corned Beef, but a good flat cut will slice up nice and evenly and is great, too. Really, look them over and buy one with enough fat and lots of lean. The slow cooking will render them both tender. Happy Corned Beef Day any day of the year.

—Gay G.

Ingredients

3-4 pounds corned beef
2 bay leaves
Packet of seasoning included in the corned beef
1 can of beer (your choice, light, dark, Stout, etc.)
3 medium peeled Russet potatoes, cut into thirds
1 small package baby carrots or 4 carrots cut into 2-inch pieces (scrubbed, not peeled)
1 onion peeled and quartered
1 medium head green cabbage
1 cube melted butter (to serve)

## *Directions*

Place Corned Beef Brisket into a large slow cooker. Add bay leaves, seasoning package, and beer. Cover and cook on low for 4 hours. Add potatoes, carrots, and onion and continue cooking for another 4 hours or until meat is tender and veggies are done. During the last hour of cooking, place cabbage, cut into 6-8 wedges, on top, cover, and cook on high for that last hour. Check occasionally and add ½ can more beer if you need more liquid. When ready to serve, remove meat to a platter. Drain liquid off of vegetables, remove bay leaves, and place in serving dish or arrange on a platter around the brisket. Pour melted butter over all of the vegetables (1 cube melted butter) and season with salt and pepper (careful not to over salt). Slice meat across the grain. Serve with mustard and/or vinegar on the side.

Serves 4

## *BRAISED LAMB SHANKS*

This is another recipe from the Basque region. It's easy to make and is quite a sophisticated dish. You can also make it with pork shanks. They will be larger than the lamb shanks so you can reduce the number you cook, depending on how many you're serving and the size of their appetites. Don't cut back too much or you might have grumbling guests. They are that good! Serve with garlic mashed potatoes because you will want something to absorb the wonderful sauce this recipe makes.

—Gay G.

## *Ingredients*

4 lamb shanks (1 per person)
3 Tablespoon olive oil (more if you need it)
3 medium-sized carrots
3 stalks of celery
1 medium onion
3 cloves garlic
1 16-ounce can stewed tomatoes
1½ cups of dry red wine
1 cup beef broth
1 teaspoon salt
1 teaspoon black pepper
½ teaspoon fresh, ground, or crushed thyme (Fresh herbs are always better if you have them. Use more when fresh.)
1 Tablespoon chopped fresh parsley (dried parsley is about a waste of time to use…no flavor)

## *Directions*

In a deep, heavy pot, like a ceramic Dutch oven, brown shanks in olive oil. Be sure to turn and brown on all sides. The more browning, the better the sauce! Remove to a plate.

While meat is browning, scrub or peel carrots and cut into chunks. A small package of baby carrots works well and is quick and easy, too. Clean and cut celery and onion into med chunks. After removing the meat when finished browning, add vegetables to the meat pot and cook on medium heat, stirring to coat, about 3 minutes. Lower heat, cover, and allow veggies to "sweat" 2-3 minutes. Sweating your vegetables like this helps to develop the flavors.

Return meat to the Dutch oven with vegetables. Be sure to include any juices that are on the meat plate. Add wine, beef broth, and seasonings. Cover and cook on low 3-4 hrs. until the meat is very tender. It's done when it starts falling off the bone.

Serve with the garlic mashed potatoes, salad, crusty French bread…and, if you like, a glass of good red wine!

# *TEXAS STYLE SHANKS*

This recipe is a different style of lamb shanks. The flavor and sauce are rich and deep with seasonings. After a visit back here to the ranch, my daughter from Idaho went to her favorite restaurant famed for their lamb shanks. We had lamb shanks while she was here, and she was craving them. My kids grew up eating lamb in Nevada when we ranched there for over 2 decades. She called me that evening after dining there and told me "Their shanks didn't hold a candle to yours!" Even folks who aren't fond of lamb are likely to enjoy these.

You can start these on top of the stove and transfer to a crockpot if you like.

—Dea

## *Ingredients*

2 Tablespoon of olive oil
4 lamb shanks
1 onion, chopped
4 cloves of garlic, minced
Salt and pepper
½ cup of red salsa
2 cups of beef broth or the equivalent
1 cup of dry red wine
2 teaspoon of cinnamon
1 Tablespoon of Italian seasoning
¼ cup of berry type juice such as cranberry or a cranberry mixture
1 stick of butter chopped up and cold

## *Directions*

Season shanks with salt and pepper.
In Dutch oven brown the shanks with the onion, add the garlic the last couple of minutes, making sure the shanks are a nice rich brown color.
Add the rest of the ingredients, and mix well, making sure the meat is coated.
Reduce heat to low and cover tightly, or place in crockpot.
Cook 'til the meat almost falls off the bone, but not quite. It should be around 2 to 3 hours on the stovetop and about 5 to 6 hours in the crockpot on low.
Remove the meat and place on a platter to stay warm.
Pour cooking liquor (the meat broth) into a saucepan and cook on high heat until it has reduced about 1/3.

Whisk in the butter until the sauce is smooth. Turn off heat.
Place shanks on a platter and cover with sauce.
Offer any leftover sauce on the side.

## *BEST BRISKET*

Brisket is a beef cut that has been a staple for feeding a large group of people for years, and many folks previously unfamiliar with it are buying it. In many respects, it is the Prime Rib of the South and Southwest. Before we had a smoker that made smoking easy, I made it in the oven. I'd marinate it overnight then slowly cook it in the oven for several hours at a low temp. It was always good and fed a bunch of people, but not near as good as a real smoked brisket. I bought my husband an electric smoker from a farm supply chain store and that was probably one of the best gifts I've ever given him. It was a great gift for me, too. Now, he loves to smoke briskets, ribs, and even the Thanksgiving turkey. But we've learned a few things I will include in the recipes. As always, don't be afraid to tailor the flavors and seasonings to please you and whoever is lucky enough to enjoy your efforts.

We prefer to buy a whole brisket, the untrimmed version sometimes called the packer brisket. It is really large, maybe even up to 18 or 20 lbs. It will have a lot more fat on it than the flat cut; it is usually untrimmed and costs less. Buy the best grade you can find, Choice, Certified Angus; never buy Select. Select grade will be missing the marbling that needs to be deep in the meat to make it moist and delectable. We will usually cut it into 3 large pieces, rather than the traditional 2 pieces. If we don't need to cook all the pieces, we wrap and freeze what we don't need. We will remove some of the fat, but, not all, ever. That's why we don't buy flat cut brisket, it often has too much fat removed, and your brisket can end up dry and rather chewy. Excess fat can always be removed before serving, but tough cuts like brisket especially need that fat to self-baste in while being cooked.

The recipe below is for one of the three pieces we would cook; just adjust the recipe for whatever size brisket roast you are cooking.

—Dea

### *Ingredients*

5-6 pound brisket roast
¼ cup salt
¼ cup brown sugar
2 Tablespoon garlic powder
1 Tablespoon onion powder
1 Tablespoon paprika
1 teaspoon cumin powder
1 Tablespoon chile powder
1 cup of fruit juice like pomegranate, apple, or cherry

## *Directions*

Mix the dry ingredients in a small bowl and then sprinkle and rub into the meat, covering all the surfaces. I like to do this and let the meat sit for a while to reach room temperature. Preheat the smoker to 250 degrees using your favorite hardwood or fruitwood or chips. Place the meat on the rack fat-side up and smoke for about 4 hours. Then remove from smoker and place in a pan or electric roaster preheated to 250 degrees. Pour in fruit juice to cover the bottom of the pan then cover the pan with foil or replace the lid on the roaster. Continue to cook for another 2 hours or more. Remove from oven and let stand. You can now slice the brisket or chop it. Pour the liquid over the meat before serving, and offer barbeque sauce for those who like it. Save any juice you haven't used from the meat, you will want to add it to any leftover meat you refrigerate or freeze. It makes heating up the meat much easier and better, without drying it out.

# *HATCH GREEN CHICKEN ENCHILADAS*

Keeping close to our N.M. culture, these enchiladas are made using Hatch Green Chiles. Check your local stores; they should be available. But, if you're less fortunate than the folks living in the Land of Enchantment, you can substitute Ortega chiles or other types of canned green chiles. They'll be delicious, too. Check the cans for the degree of heat: hot, medium, or mild. Choose the type your crew will like the best, keeping in mind that chiles can't be trusted. I've bought mild chiles that burned a hole right through my mouth and hot chiles that went down like water. It's a game of Chile Roulette, but definitely a game worth playing!

—Gay G.

## *Ingredients*

1 cup chopped onion
2 cloves fresh garlic, minced
4 Tablespoon olive or vegetable oil
4 cups chopped cooked chicken
2 jars or cans (7-8 oz. each) green chile salsa or green enchilada sauce
3 small cans chopped Hatch green chiles
1 Tablespoon flour
4 chicken bouillon cubes crumbled or equivalent chicken stock base
2 cups milk
1 cup heavy whipping cream
3 cups shredded Monterrey Jack cheese
12 corn tortillas (about 7-inch size)
Sour cream

## *Directions*

Sauté garlic and onion in ½ the oil until tender. Add chicken, green chile salsa, chopped green chiles and cook on low until heated through then turn off heat. In a saucepan, combine flour and chicken bouillon. Over medium heat, slowly whisk in milk, stirring constantly until mixture starts to bubble and thicken slightly. Remove from heat and stir in half of the cheese. Stir until cheese has melted and mixture is smooth. Set aside.

Heat tortillas one at a time in remaining oil and cook on both sides until soft and pliable. Set each on a paper towel to drain while finishing other tortillas. Dip each cooked tortilla in the sauce until well coated. Place on a flat plate and fill with a generous amount of chicken. Sprinkle a bit of cheese over the chicken then roll the tortilla and place in large baking dish seam side down. When baking dish is full, cover with more sauce, sprinkle with cheese, cover with foil.

Bake in preheated 350-degree oven for 15 minutes. Remove foil and cook 5-10 minutes more. To serve, dish 2-3 enchiladas onto a plate and garnish with sour cream.

Serves 4-6

## MARSALA FOR 4

This recipe is a great example of a dish you will likely find in an Italian or a more up-scale type restaurant. It is so delicious and fit for a special night or dinner party, but is simple to prepare. Look for dry Marsala to make this, the sweet version is better for desserts. This Marsala recipe doesn't require the use of pasta, though you can always plate it on pasta. The recipe can also be doubled.

You can use the more traditional veal if it is available, or chicken breast. But I must mention quail. It is so good, really makes an over-the-top dinner! Simply fry/sauté your quail after dredging like you would the chicken or veal 'til golden brown. Then pour a little of the butter/oil mixture you fried it in over the quail and bake at 400 degrees for 20 minutes, and set that pan aside. After the quail is done, proceed with the recipe. I do omit the lemon when using quail. The mushrooms lend themselves to the earthy flavor of the quail. Figure on 2 quail per person.

If you use chicken, you will want to slice your chicken breast in half by butterflying it. To do this, place your hand flat on the breast, but have your fingers pointed upward. Take your knife and slice the breast horizontally under your hand, stopping before you cut all the way through. Open the breast and finish cutting it into 2 pieces. Place plastic wrap over the pieces and use either a rolling pin or a mallet and beat the chicken until very thin, around ⅛ to ¼ inch thick.

—Dea

## Ingredients

2 boneless chicken breasts cut and pounded into 4 pieces or 4 veal cutlets
1 cup of flour
Salt and pepper
4 Tablespoon of olive oil
3 Tablespoon butter
½ pound sliced mushrooms
2 cloves minced garlic
About ¾ cup of dry Marsala
About ¾ cup of chicken broth
¼ to ½ cup of heavy cream (depending upon your preference)
Fresh lemon or lemon juice
Parmesan cheese

## Directions for Chicken or Veal

Prepare 2 chicken breasts as described above or use 4 veal cutlets.
Dredge the cutlets, or pounded chicken breasts, in flour seasoned with salt and pepper.
Heat olive oil and butter 'til it shimmers. (shimmer is the method of knowing a lower heat fat has reached the correct temp.)
Place 2 of the chicken breasts or cutlets in the oil, cook 'til golden brown on both sides.
Set cooked pieces aside on a platter in a warm place and then continue cooking all the pieces and adding them to the platter.
Keep the pan on medium-high heat, adding more butter if necessary.
Add mushrooms, cook until beginning to brown.
Add minced garlic; allow to cook 1 minute.
Add the Marsala, stirring to loosen any bits leftover. from the meat.
Add chicken broth; allow to simmer about 10 to 15 minutes; it should reduce some and begin to thicken.
Add ¼ to ½ cup of heavy cream, and place the chicken back into the pan.
Allow to cook a few minutes, spooning sauce over meat.
You may add a grind of black pepper, a squeeze of fresh lemon and a sprinkle of Parmesan when plating.

# *LEMON CREAM PASTA*

Pasta, of any kind, is my favorite thing to eat. A diet that strictly forbids pasta is off my list! That doesn't mean you have to overdo it and eat spaghetti for breakfast, lunch, and dinner every day (would that really be so bad?), but good pasta now and then just makes life worth living. Understanding that it is really the sauce that makes pasta so wonderful, at the very least, we put it on our favorite vegetables.

These days pasta has grown up. There are pasta sauces for every taste preference and budget. Its versatility is only limited by your imagination. This recipe for Lemon Cream Pasta evolved in my kitchen over time and is rooted in the Cream Pasta we used to have at least once a week growing up. I love lemons, I love cream, and I love pasta so marrying the three together was probably inevitable. Besides being delicious, it is quick to make, easy, and inexpensive, but your guests/family won't suspect any of that. I have served this dish many times at the ranch without one cowboy complaint!

—Gay G.

## *Ingredients*

1 pound dry spaghetti or linguini
2 cups whipping cream
¼ to ½ cup fresh lemon juice (depending on the lemons, you can even use more)
¾ tsp salt
1 cup grated Parmesan cheese
1 teaspoon lemon zest
1 small package frozen petite green beans

## *Directions*

Bring a large pot of water to boil (don't forget to salt the water)
Add pasta and reduce heat to medium-high to keep boiling. Stir to prevent pasta from sticking. While water is heating and the pasta is cooking, combine cream, lemon juice, zest, and salt. Stir and set aside. The lemon juice will cause the cream to thicken while it's resting. Taste the cream and add more lemon if you don't have enough flavor. Some lemons are very acidic and tart so you can add a pinch or two of sugar to soften the taste. It's legal this time because you can't bet on the lemons. Meyer lemons are the best choice, if they are available.
Rinse the green beans under warm water just to thaw. About 3 minutes before pasta will be done, add beans and continue cooking until pasta is al dente and beans are still bright green. Drain pasta and beans in a strainer. Place in a large pasta bowl and pour cream mixture over. Toss well. Add grated parmesan cheese, toss again, and serve with extra cheese. Garnish with a little chopped parsley (optional).

Serves 4 generously

### *Seafood variations*

Sautee shrimp, scallops, or a combination in olive oil/butter and garlic. Set aside and add to finished pasta just before serving. Talk about stepping up the game, this version is 5-Star. You can also just drop cleaned thawed shrimp into the boiling pasta water right after the beans go in and cook until shrimp is white. Be sure to not overcook or the shrimp will be tough. If using precooked shrimp, thaw and add to boiling pasta water about 2 minutes before pasta is done cooking.

*Serving suggestion*: Crusty French bread and butter, tossed green salad with vinaigrette dressing.

# RANCH BOLOGNESE

This is my clean-out-the-freezer recipe. I always save small amounts of leftover cooked meats, everything from chicken to steaks, lamb, sausage, etc. This recipe is based on the old Italian Gravy or Bolognese. I usually save small bits of vegetables to use in this or soups I may throw together. When you live a long way from a grocery store, you save everything so it will be on hand when you decide you want to make something. I even freeze raw mushrooms that aren't as fresh as they should be to use in this or to make another sauce.

You can use raw meats such as ground beef, sausage, stew meat, etc. if you want to. You don't have to use all pre-cooked meats and I often mix the two, using both cooked and uncooked meats. Rotisserie chicken, leftover steak or roast, lamb, beef, pork cuts, all work well to add great flavor and richness. Because this is made from a wide range of natural ingredients and whatever meats you have on hand, it will never come out exactly the same, but it will always come out delicious and satisfying. Any time you are cooking with natural products; fruits, vegetables, and meats, there will be a variance in taste, and often texture.

This sauce freezes very well, I love having it on hand. It makes a delicious lasagna, is great over pasta, or egg or vegetable noodles, or mashed potatoes or rice.

Warning, the smell of this sauce cooking may draw in strangers, neighbors, husbands, and cowboys.

—Dea

Ingredients

¼ cup olive oil
1 cup chopped onion
1 cup chopped celery
¼ cup of raw, chopped bacon ends
Uncooked meat you may want to use, from ½ to 1 pound such as sausage or ground beef or even diced stew meat, short ribs or lamb ribs
2 to 3 cloves of minced garlic
Cooked, chopped leftover meats
Chopped leftover veggies such as squash, eggplant, etc.
2 1-pound cans of diced tomatoes
1 1-pound can of tomato sauce
2 Tablespoon of Italian seasoning, or your own preference of Italian herbs
1 Tablespoon of Worcestershire sauce
1 teaspoon of red pepper flakes

Black pepper
2 cups of chicken broth
¼ cup of milk
½ cup of dry grated Parmesan or Romano
1 Tablespoon of wine vinegar
½ cup of Chardonnay
A pinch of sugar

## Directions

In a large pot or Dutch oven, place the olive oil, chopped onion, and celery, sauté 'til soft.
Remove vegetables from pan, leaving oil, add ¼ cup of chopped bacon ends, and whatever uncooked (raw) meat you may want to use, from ½ to 1 lb. Cook 'til browned but not cooked through. Return the sautéed vegetables to the pan and the cloves of minced garlic; stir and cook for 2 to 3 minutes.

## Add:

Chopped leftover meats, amount dependent on how heavy and robust a meat sauce is desired
Finely chopped leftover or fresh vegetables like squash, eggplant, spinach, etc.
Cans of diced tomatoes
Can of tomato sauce
Italian seasoning, or your own preference of Italian herbs
Worcestershire sauce
Red pepper flakes
Black pepper
Chicken broth
Adjust the seasoning after adding the broth to avoid over salting the sauce; many of the ingredients already contain salt.
You can move this to a slow cooker now if you like, or let cook covered on the stove at very low heat for several hours, stirring occasionally and adding a small amount of water if needed. The longer it cooks, the more flavors will develop, and everything will break down to a smoother consistency. Taste occasionally as it gets closer to being finished to adjust the seasonings, bearing in mind some flavors become concentrated and others weaken.
About an hour before serving remove any meat you added with bones, dice the meat, return to the pot, and throw away the bones. Add the milk, dry grated Parmesan or Romano, red wine vinegar, Chardonnay, and a pinch of sugar. Cook for 45 minutes or longer to mellow the flavors.
Serve over desired pasta or other base topped with freshly grated Parmesan, Asiago, or whatever aged, sharp cheese is preferred; or freeze the Bolognese in containers for later use. This makes a wonderful sauce for so many things.

## *CHICKEN FRIED STEAK NEW MEXICO STYLE*

Located in the Rio Grande Valley lies the little town of Hatch, N.M., home of the Hatch Green Chile. This Chile is considered a staple in N.M., ranking right up there with milk, flour, sugar, eggs, and coffee. No respectable kitchen is ever without some source of Hatch Greens. New Mexicans can make just about anything better using their beloved green chile.

Pie Town, N.M., a community of less than 200 people, is famous for, you guessed it: PIE! One just about has to be on their way to somewhere to go through Pie Town, but once you get there you just have to stop and have a piece of pie. Visitors can get an assortment of pies including the Hatch Green Chile Apple Pie. It may sound crazy, but it is actually delicious.

New Mexicans make a green chile version of just about everything including my favorite Chicken Fried Steak. At one local diner, they serve a 4 oz. or 8 oz. Fiesta Chicken Fried Steak with their own green chile sauce. It's over the top good and is on the "tour" when friends and family come to visit. It ranks right up there with the White Sands National Monument, Three-Rivers Petroglyphs, Smokey Bear Museum (where Smokey is buried), and Billy the Kid's stomping grounds. There is a lot to see…and eat…in these parts of New Mexico.

Chicken Fried Steak is one of those real comfort foods and making it at home isn't hard. The key to success is a good heavy Dutch oven or cast-iron skillet. You need to be able to heat the oil hot enough to get a good crunchy brown coating when the meat is cooking. Light weight pans, especially Teflon coated ones, just won't do the trick.

The second secret to success is to soak the meat overnight or for several hours in, guess what, buttermilk! Yes, one more way to use your leftover buttermilk after you've made your own delicious homemade Ranch or Blue Cheese salad dressing. Give our New Mexico Style Chicken Fried Steak a try and your crew will be crowing your praises!

Before you start, here's a word about gravy. It's NOT that hard to make, but it scares many a good cook to death. We've all heard the horror stories about the cook whose gravy looked like "paste". Maybe you know that story all too well, but take heart because gravy making is EASY. It just takes practice. If you ruin a batch, try it again. Eventually, you'll find out that it's almost impossible to make bad gravy once you get the hang of it. Remember, a little gravy can cover a multitude of sins or even melt a cowboy's heart.

—Gay G.

## Ingredients

2 pound cube steaks or round steak cut into 6-8 pieces and pounded to ½ inch thick. You can ask the meat counter attendant to run it through the tenderizing machine to save you time but first look in the meat case where cube steaks are commonly packaged and available.
2 cups buttermilk or enough to cover the meat in a shallow baking dish
2 cups flour
3 teaspoon salt
3 teaspoon black pepper
2 teaspoon garlic powder
1 teaspoon baking soda
1 teaspoon baking powder
4 eggs

Crisco or lard melted in pan to be 1-2 inches deep (or more if you prefer) You can also use liquid vegetable oil. Olive oil will have a distinct flavor and is not as well suited for this dish. To "shallow fry" you want at least 1 inch of oil. Add more oil as needed during cooking but be sure it's hot before adding more pieces of meat otherwise it will end up soggy and greasy. Crisp steaks are what you want!

## *Directions*

Place steaks in shallow baking dish. Add buttermilk making sure all of the meat is covered. Cover with plastic wrap and refrigerate overnight or for several hours. Turn meat at least once during soaking time.
Take pan out of refrigerator 1 hour before cooking and let set on counter to warm to room temp.
Heat oven to 250 degrees
When ready to cook steaks, heat oil on medium heat in cast iron or another heavy skillet or Dutch oven on top of the stove. In a shallow dish, mix dry ingredients (can be done in a plastic freezer bag, too). Beat eggs in another shallow bowl or dish and add ¼ cup of the buttermilk.
Dredge each piece of meat in flour to coat both sides, then in egg/milk mixture, then in flour again. Place meat in skillet, and cook until golden brown; turn and repeat. Do the same with all pieces of meat being sure to cook long enough for meat to be done. Remove and drain on cooling rack over a paper towel-lined baking sheet. Keep warm in 250-degree oven while making gravy.

## *HATCH GREEN CHILE GRAVY*

3 cups whole milk
½ cup heavy cream (optional)
3 Tablespoon flour
1 Tablespoon butter
¼ cup pan drippings (oil from cooking)
Salt and pepper to taste.
1 can diced Hatch Green Chilies (if not available substitute diced Ortega chilies) Use 2 cans if you really want a lot of chile flavor.
Dash of hot sauce to taste (optional)

When finished cooking meat drain off oil from pan but leave about ¼ cup of oil and meat drippings. To the oil in pan add 3 level Tablespoons of flour. Stir well to mix flour and oil on medium-low heat. Let cook, stirring, for a couple of minutes to well incorporate the flour and oil. Add butter. Slowly whisk in whole milk, cream, chilies, salt, and pepper. Continue stirring on low-med heat until gravy thickens and bubbles. If too thick, add more milk and stir well. Gravy will thicken more as it cools. Salt and pepper to taste. Serve hot over steaks.

# *SCALLOPED SEAFOOD FOR 4*

Everyone I know loves surf and turf, and while it used to be pretty much-considered steak and lobster, the idea is a lot broader now, encompassing almost any red meat and seafood or fish, served together. The recipe below is a favorite of mine, fit for a holiday, an anniversary or Valentine's Day dinner, any kind of special occasion. It is luscious and elegant. Of course, you may just want to serve it without beef and enjoy a special dish. I do like to serve this with prime rib or a nice rib-eye steak. You can also serve it as a main dish. When I want to have it with another main course food, I make the recipe as below, in small ramekins. If you want it as a main dish, I use small casserole or gratin dishes. The recipe can also easily be doubled. Another thing I love about this recipe is that you can assemble it ahead of time, cover it tightly, and refrigerate until the next day, this is especially helpful if you are really planning a fancy dinner. Take it out of the fridge and let stand about 20 to 25 minutes and then add the crumb mixture before broiling about 4 minutes, 'til the top is nice and golden brown.

—Dea

## *Ingredients*

2 Tablespoon butter, and another 2 Tablespoon butter and 1 Tablespoon butter, used separately
1 Tablespoon minced garlic
4 ounce of fresh sliced mushrooms
1 Tablespoon finely chopped scallion or chives
Salt & pepper
½ pound sea scallops
½ pound raw, deveined, tail removed shrimp
½ cup dry white wine
½ cup clam nectar or clam juice
½ cup heavy cream
Hot sauce such as Tabasco
Pinch of red pepper
1 Tablespoon chopped parsley
½ cup Panko or bread crumbs
2 Tablespoon grated Parmesan cheese

## *Directions*

Melt 2 Tablespoon butter in a large skillet, add sliced fresh mushrooms, sauté 4 to 5 minutes, then stir in garlic, and onion/chives. Add salt and sprinkle of black pepper, cook 1 or 2 minutes. Add sea scallops, rinsed and patted dry. Cook scallops about 2 minutes on each side, add the raw shrimp, rinsed and patted dry, also. Stir and cook for 5 minutes, shrimp should be pink and scallops just cooked. Pour in dry white wine and clam nectar or juice. Push seafood and mushrooms to the side of the pan and whisk in 2 Tablespoon or more butter and flour 'til smooth. Add heavy cream and 2 shakes of hot sauce.

Place mixture in greased or sprayed dishes.

You can now cover tightly and refrigerate, or go on to the next steps:

Melt 1 Tablespoon butter; add chopped parsley or herb of your choice, pinch of ground red pepper, like cayenne, and panko or breadcrumbs along with grated Parmesan cheese. Sprinkle the above mixture over dishes and broil for 4 to 5 minutes, 'til golden and crisp. Serve piping hot.

Let stand 5 minutes before serving and enjoy!

## SOUTHWESTERN CABBAGE ROLLS

Cabbage rolls have lots of variations, depending on what ethnic background the recipe came from. I think they're one of the most "comforting" dishes around. Almost all call for some mixture of ground meat, rice, and a sauce. This recipe is where Southwest meets old European. They are sometimes called Cabbage Tamales. It combines some great flavors, and folks who may think they don't like cabbage rolls should give these a try; they might just change their minds.

The rolls can be baked in the oven or cooked in a slow cooker for a few hours. The amount of rice has been cut down in these, making a healthier, higher protein dish. You can also add a can of drained black beans in place of the rice if you prefer. The eggs act as a binder, eliminating the need for so much rice. I know some cooks will boil the whole head of cabbage, I don't. I cut 2 to 3 inches of the core out, carefully peel off 10 to 12 leaves, and boil until I can just get them to barely bend. Overcooking the cabbage will make the rolls soggy and tend to fall apart, especially if you use the slow cooker.

—Dea

## *Ingredients*

1 pound ground beef
1 package Mexican chorizo, 6 to 8 ounce
1 onion chopped
¼ cup uncooked rice or 1 can drained black beans
2 eggs
1 head green cabbage
Flour
½ to ⅔ cup of salsa
1 teaspoon chicken base paste or 1 cube chicken bullion

## *Directions*

In a large skillet sauté ground beef and chorizo, along with the onion. Add either uncooked white rice or can of drained black beans, season with black pepper, and salt, if needed. Mix well and set aside. Boil the cabbage leaves as mentioned above, when leaves are through cooking, drain the leaves. While the leaves are draining add eggs to the cooled down meat mixture, mixing well. Place 3 to 4 Tablespoon of meat mixture in leaf and roll up like a burrito, tucking the ends under. Place in a baking pan or slow cooker, layering the rolls. Lightly sprinkle a very small amount of flour on each layer of cabbage rolls. This will work as a thickener for the sauce. Pour salsa in a small bowl; add chicken base paste or dry chicken bouillon to the salsa, mixing well. Pour over the cabbage rolls.

Cook in a crockpot on low for 4 hours or bake covered in a 350-degree oven for around an hour.

These are delicious topped with plain yogurt or sour cream. My husband will sometimes add salsa as a topping.

# *SANTA MARIA TRI-TIP BBQ*

A short hour drive north of Santa Barbara, California, is the farming community of Santa Maria, birthplace of the well-known Santa Maria Style BBQ. It was traditionally a top sirloin strip barbecued and served with beans, salad, French bread, and salsa. After a local butcher decided to "peel off" the end of the sirloin, the Tri-tip cut of meat was born and the rest is history. President Ronald Reagan was a big fan and the traditional Santa Maria Style BBQ was served several times to guests at the White House.

Now available across the U.S. (if it's not in your store's meat counter, ask for it), the Tri-tip has become a versatile retail cut of beef. It can be roasted, sliced and grilled, barbecued, or cubed for stews and soups. Whatever you choose to do with Tri-tip, it's sure to be delicious!

For the real deal, Pinquito Beans are traditional as the main side dish along with grilled crusty French bread, green salad, and mild to medium red salsa. The Pinquito is a small red bean grown in the Santa Maria region that was developed by crossing a small white bean with a pink bean variety. If Pinquitos aren't available, pinto or pink beans are acceptable substitutes, just don't overcook them. Santa Maria Style beans are never mushy!

Now a staple at family gatherings, fund-raisers, company parties, etc., it's become the go-to meal for California ranch brandings. There's a popular rancher saying that if you get invited to more than one branding on a given weekend, go to the one that serves the best food! That's good advice, since you're not going to get paid for the privilege of working cattle all day in the dust or mud and muck, but you're sure to be fed well. That's how we treat our friends! Come along, saddle-up, and let's get cooking a Santa Maria Style BBQ for your next branding (i.e. gathering) of friends and family.

—Gay G.

### *Ingredients*

Beef Tri-Tips, as many as you need. One will serve 4-5 people.
Salt, pepper, and garlic powder

### *Directions*

Season meat liberally with garlic powder, salt, and pepper. Let stand 30 minutes before cooking. Grill on high heat to sear, turning once, until a good brown is seen. Lower heat to medium/low and continue cooking until meat hits desired doneness (use meat thermometer to check). You don't want to overcook, as well-done beef will be less tender, flavorful, and juicy. It will take 30-45 minutes for the tri-tip to be done, depending on size and heat temperature. Let it set (rest) uncovered for 5 minutes before slicing. Cut across the grain for the best eating experience.

For a fun event, dress up your table with red or blue bandana napkins, mason jars for wine or iced tea glasses, and a rustic candle centerpiece. Your guests will feel like they just came in off the range!

Note: If you have leftover Tri-tip, you can slice thin and make delicious Tri-tip sandwiches the next day. At most ranch brandings you'll see 4-8 Tri-tips on the grill and a pot of beans so big it takes a couple strong men to lift it. That's a gathering!

Enjoy! And now that you've done the Santa Maria Style BBQ, get creative with other ways to use this versatile cut of beef. Be fearless...keep cook'n.

## *BEEF STROGANOFF*

Beef Stroganoff is an old recipe, and not seen as much as it once was. Despite the current loss of popularity, this is a great real food and can be a Keto type dish. No, you don't have to serve it over noodles or mashed potatoes, but you can if you like. It is also a great way to use leftover sirloin steak, if that ever happens at your house. You'll simply add the precooked, sliced meat after adding the yogurt or sour cream. Grilled steak will add a nice slightly smoky flavor.

—Dea

In a large skillet:
Brown 1 pound of thinly sliced sirloin steak in 1 to 2 Tablespoon oil, then remove to a plate
Add to hot skillet:
1 Tablespoon butter
1 medium onion thinly sliced
Cook 'til the onion is translucent

Add:
About ½ pound of sliced mushrooms and cook 'til beginning to brown

Add:
2 minced cloves of garlic
Cook for a minute or two, 'til the garlic smells sweet

Add:
1 cup beef consommé or beef broth
¼ cup of Burgundy wine (optional)
Cook for 5 minutes

Stir in:
1 cup sour cream or plain Greek yogurt
Add cooked beef strips and allow to thicken to desired consistency, but do not boil.
If a thicker consistency is desired, flour dissolved in a small amount of cold water may be added.

Serves 4

## *SEMI-SMOKED TURKEY*

My family prefers a lighter smoke taste when it comes to fowl. We came up with this recipe for turkey, which makes a slightly smoky, moist, and tender turkey. It is super easy and doesn't require a lot of basting or attention while you're preparing the rest of the meal. Don't be afraid of putting a heavy coating of the spices. Turkey is a fairly bland meat and benefits from seasonings.

—Dea

### *Ingredients*

12 to 18 pound turkey
Seasoning salt
Garlic salt
Onion salt
Lemon pepper
Red chile powder
Black pepper
2 oranges cut into quarters
2 lemons cut into quarters
Butter or oil

### *Directions*

Preheat smoker to 250 degrees
Remove turkey from packaging over sink; discard wrapping
Remove any giblets and reserve for later use in soups or gravies
Run cold water through the turkey's cavity and over the bird
Pat dry with paper towels
Place turkey on a cookie sheet
Salt and pepper the inside of the bird, and stuff the citrus pieces into the cavity.
Cover the bird with oil or butter.
Sprinkle the seasoning on the bird one at a time. You will have a layer of each seasoning.
Place bird without the sheet in the smoker for 1 hour, 1½ hours if you are using a larger bird.
When done smoking, place turkey in a roasting pan in a preheated 350-degree oven for approximately 1 hour, covered. After 1 hour, remove covering to allow browning. Keep roasting the bird. When bird has reached 165 degrees and has a pretty golden color, remove from oven. Remove and discard the citrus fruit pieces. Cover the turkey loosely and allow it to stand for at least ½ hour before carving.

## *TERIYAKI FLANK STEAK*

Flank steak is often used in the classic London Broil, but we think this Teriyaki style has much more flavor appeal. There is some do-ahead prep time to make the marinade, but the actual cooking time is quick and easy. Serve it with the rice/vermicelli pilaf (see Sharon's Rice Pilaf) that can also be made ahead of time and you'll have a crowd-pleasing hit.

—Gay G.

Ingredients

½ cup soy sauce
2 Tablespoon brown sugar
2 Tablespoon Worcestershire sauce
1 Tablespoon white vinegar
¾ teaspoon ground ginger
2 garlic cloves minced or ¼ teaspoon garlic powder
1½ – 2 pounds beef flank steak

Instructions
Make the marinade by combining the first 6 ingredients in a small bowl. Place flank steak in shallow dish or baking pan, pour marinade over, and cover with plastic wrap. Marinate at least 6 hours and up to 24 hrs. turning once or twice.
Place meat on broiling pan, score diagonally to keep it flat, and broil 5 minutes on each side for medium-rare. Rest 2 minutes, slice across the grain in 1-inch pieces. Steak can also be cooked on an outside grill over medium-high heat for the same time period.
Serves 4

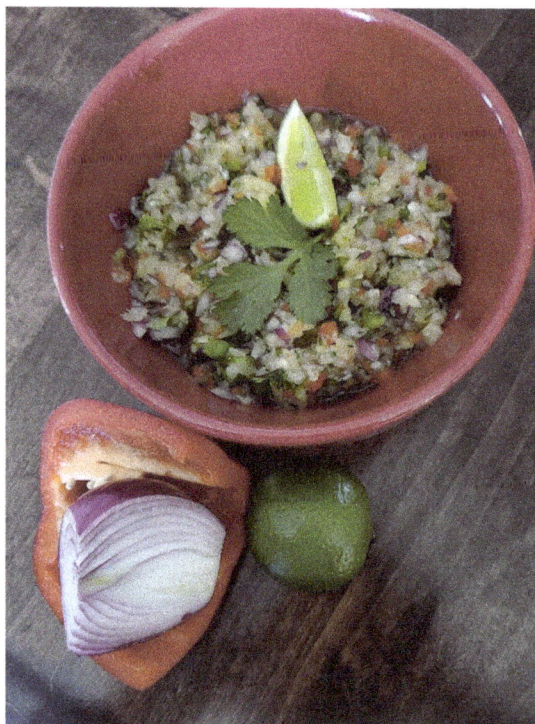

## *PANIOLO SHRIMP TACOS WITH PINEAPPLE SALSA*

Tacos are always a treat and if you make a Taco Bar, everyone can customize their own. That's a big win for the cook. The Pineapple Salsa gives them an island style, so we named our Shrimp Taco version after the cowboys of Hawaii, the Paniolos. (Some say Paniolas.)

The Paniolos have a rich history in ranching and carry on many of the traditions of the Spanish Vaqueros that have been passed down from their early training in cattle handling and horsemanship. Probably the most famous Hawaiian ranch is the Parker Ranch on the Big Island of Hawaii. Started by John Parker, who married the granddaughter of King Kamehameha, the Parker Ranch grew to 250,000 acres and became the largest privately owned ranch in the U.S.

Today the Paniolos continue to ranch and promote the Hawaiian cowboy culture with their music, dress, and western tack. Each year the Parker Ranch hosts two rodeos where visitors can watch the Paniolos compete in ranching events. Several ranches on the islands, including the Parker Ranch, have tours and visitor centers so next time you visit Hawaii, go a little "cowboy."

—Gay G.

## Ingredients

1 pound cooked shrimp with tails off
12 corn tortillas
Vegetable oil for frying
2 Tablespoon butter
1 can crushed pineapple (about 8 ounce) undrained
1 medium red bell pepper finely chopped
1 cup red onion finely chopped
1 jalapeno pepper finely chopped
½ cup chopped cilantro
½ teaspoon salt
⅓ head of green cabbage shredded or chopped finely
½ cup sour cream
¼ cup heavy whipping cream
2-3 limes

## Directions

Make the salsa first so it has a couple of hours to allow the flavors to set. Mix the pineapple, red pepper, red onion, jalapeno, cilantro, and salt together. Set aside.

Make the Crema by mixing sour cream and heavy cream with a pinch of salt and a good squeeze of lime juice (about 3 tsp).

Cook tortillas in oil on medium-high heat, folding to form the taco shell. Cook to crisp texture, drain on paper towels while preparing shrimp. You can keep them warm in a low oven if you wish. If you prefer softer taco shells, wrap corn tortillas in a towel and microwave for a minute or so to warm.

Rinse shrimp and pat dry with paper towels. Chop coarsely. Melt 2 Tablespoon butter in a pan and sauté shrimp just until hot (about 2 minutes max). Transfer from pan to a serving bowl.

To assemble tacos, fill taco shells with layers as follows: shrimp, cabbage, pineapple salsa, and drizzle top with crema. Serve with lime wedges.

Don't forget to try the Taco Bar idea. It's fun and a time saver. As they say in Hawaiian, "le'ale'a" (Enjoy!)

Serves 4

# SMOKED PORK RIBS

Pork ribs smoked are delicious, whether you prefer St. Louis ribs, spareribs, or baby back ribs. The St. Louis style are larger, meatier, and a little fatter. We prefer a slightly sweet, smoky flavor since pork benefits from sweet flavors and herbs. The easiest way to make sure they are tender and done is by checking that the meat has shrunk back from the ends of the bone. There are lots of dry rub mixes you can simply buy off the grocery shelf, but we prefer to make our own, and I've included a basic one. You might try buying some rubs to see what flavors you prefer and then re-create your own.

There is a large variety of bottled barbeque sauces you can purchase, or you can use your own to baste the ribs the last hour and a half. Some folks prefer to baste the ribs with apple juice. You can try the various BBQ sauce varieties in the stores until you find what you like- hotter, sweeter, etc. Then make your own signature sauce to complement the rub.

—Dea

## Ingredients

1 full rack of pork ribs
½ cup of brown sugar
2 Tablespoon onion salt
2 Tablespoon garlic salt
1 Tablespoon lemon pepper
1 Tablespoon Italian seasoning
1 teaspoon black pepper
1 teaspoon cayenne pepper
1 teaspoon paprika
BBQ sauce

## Directions

Mix the above dry ingredients and sprinkle over the ribs and rub into the meat. Preheat smoker to 250 degrees. When smoker has reached 250 degrees place ribs on rack, fat side up. Smoke for 3 hours. Then baste with either apple juice or sauce every half hour, while smoking for another 2 to 3 hours. Ribs are done when the meat pulls back from the ends of the bones and they have reached 165 degrees.

# *THYME FOR STEW*

Everyone needs a good stew recipe. Stew is a staple. This recipe is over the top delicious and will please even a stew snob or a stew hater, if there is such a thing. My sister, Kathy, made it for some of her friends and me when we were all visiting her at the California ranch. We couldn't stop raving and proclaiming it to be the best stew we'd ever eaten. Yes, definitely serve it to guests and don't think they'll feel cheated. This is an authentic gourmet stew and easy to make.

—Gay G.

## *Ingredients*

1 Tablespoon Olive oil
2 pounds trimmed and cubed chuck roast (cut large pieces)
2 teaspoon black pepper
1½ teaspoon salt
6 cloves chopped garlic
1 cup dry red wine
2 cups unsalted or low salt beef broth
3 Tablespoon flour
2 Tablespoon tomato paste
4 sprigs fresh thyme (or 1 ½ teaspoon dried – fresh is better)
2 bay leaves
1 pound small turnips peeled and cubed - about 3 cups (or substitute potatoes for all or half of turnips)
1 pound carrots (scrub clean, no need to peel) and cut in 1-inch pieces or use 1 pound cleaned baby carrots)
2 cups celery, washed and cut into 1-inch pieces
8 ounce (about 2 cups) frozen pearl onions
1 cup washed small fresh button mushrooms
1 cup water
2 Tablespoon chopped flat parsley

## *Directions*

Heat oven to 350 degrees. Heat oil in a Dutch oven over medium heat, and brown meat that has been seasoned with half of the pepper and salt. Be sure to brown well to get a good glaze on the meat and drippings in the pan. Remove to plate. When all meat is browned, add garlic and cook 1 minute stirring constantly. Add wine and cook about 2 minutes, stirring to loosen browning and incorporate into liquid. Whisk together beef stock and flour until there are no lumps. Whisk into wine mixture and simmer on medium-low heat until it begins to thicken. Add tomato paste and remaining herbs and seasonings. Return meat to pot; cover with a lid, and cook in oven for 45 minutes. Remove, add vegetables, return to oven and cook covered for additional 45 minutes or until vegetables and meat are tender. Garnish with parsley to serve.

Slow cook method: Instead of returning meat to the original pot, put everything in a slow cooker (including vegetables) and cook on low heat for 6 hrs. or high for 3 hrs. Test this time and adjust accordingly, cooking just until meat and vegetables are tender, but not too soft. You can turn it off and reheat to serve when ready.

### *REAL COWBOY SPAGHETTI & STORY*

The state of Nevada is widely known for its gambling, big hotels, entertainment, and Las Vegas nightlife, but that is such a small part of the story. It was brought into the U.S. as a state in 1864 to supply silver to the Union Forces during the Civil War and was tagged the "Battle Born" state. Before the gambling and all the glitz of Las Vegas, there was and still is the Nevada of mining and ranching. A harsh land of beautiful deserts and tall mountain peaks, this Great Basin state developed the reputation of producing individuals as tough and resilient as the land itself.

Many of those who came were immigrants from the "old countries" of Italy, Spain, Switzerland, and France. They took up the work they had known in their homelands: cattle and sheep ranching, dairy production, and farming. After the long Atlantic boat ride and a slow train or buggy ride across the U.S., they were probably "Tough Enough" by the time they reached the sagebrush land of Nevada. At any rate, they settled, developed their own communities, bought land, and thrived, developing some of the most successful agriculture operations in the state and contributing to its great history.

In 2013, the National Cowboy Poetry Gathering in Elko, Nevada, coordinated with the Western Folklife Center to feature Italian Buckaroos: Old World & New World, which spotlighted the rich legacy of Italian American ranching in the American West. Nevada's buckaroo and ranch history is rich with the legacy of the Italian cowboys and, may I say, real spaghetti.

Have you ever searched the internet for "Cowboy Spaghetti"? Probably not, that is not a common search topic. Just for fun, I did the search, and was I ever surprised to find all kinds of recipes under that title. They're interesting, to say the least! They have ingredients like bacon, beer, hot sauce, Cheddar cheese, and kidney beans. That's fine, I guess. You must forgive me, but on this subject of spaghetti sauce (the red kind), I'm a bit of a purest. Granted there are many styles of sauces made in Italy and they are regional. I like them all, but one is never confused about whether it is Italian spaghetti sauce or not. I promise you; it does not contain kidney beans or cheddar cheese.

American Italians sometimes call it gravy, which has been the subject of debate for a long time. Some think the term gravy was adopted to try to fit in, but as an American Italian, I think gravy was just the English term they took up when learning the language. Trying to fit in just does not make sense from my experience. As for cowboys eating spaghetti, I'm an expert on that. Check these last names of the ranchers and cowboys I grew up around: Gardella, Baroli, Ferretto, Gabarino, Rosachi, Avansino, Pagni, Lagomarsino, Capurro, and there are more. Do you see a common denominator? Like Al Capone, their names all end in vowels. Very Italian! Unlike Capone, they weren't mobsters. They were all from ranching families in Nevada and were the "gang" of friends and relatives my dad grew up, ranched, and rodeoed with in his younger years.
Spaghetti was a staple in all their households, as it was in mine growing up. Big lunches were common, and a big platter of spaghetti always took center stage every day.

Nonna Baroli (it means Grandmother Baroli) raised six Baroli boys on their ranch south of Reno. Every morning she would make breakfast for them all then clean up the kitchen. As soon as she finished the breakfast chores, she started on the lunch. The big meal of the day, it always included a huge plate of pasta. Lunch was ready when "the boys" and her husband came in from work. To make this story more impressive, consider that Nonna Baroli grew her own tomatoes and made her own tomato paste for her sauce. That's a bit humbling to we modern cooks. In my own defense, I buy imported Italian canned tomatoes and tomato sauce. That's somewhat redeeming; right?

Here is a little side story about Nonna Baroli that I always found adorable. Her husband had built her a kitchen in the basement of the house. The summer days in northern Nevada can be hot, they had no cooling or air conditioning in those days, and you can imagine what all that cooking for those Baroli men did to the temperature in her kitchen. To remedy this problem, her husband had built the kitchen in the basement where it was naturally cooler. In the summer, she would do her cooking down there.

One day her granddaughter, Dolores Baroli Gardella, came home from school in the wintertime. She went to find her grandmother. When Nonna was finally located, she was cooking in the basement, unusual for that time of the year. That day Dolores's Nonna was very upset. You see, she was a terrible baker! She could not make a cake to save her soul. That day she was down in the basement hiding from everyone while she tried to bake a successful cake. When I have some big flop in the kitchen, I think of Nonna Baroli and her cake fiasco. It makes me laugh…and then I make spaghetti.

A word about making red pasta sauce, it is never going to taste the same two times in a row regardless of what recipe you use. There are so many variables starting with the tomatoes. Some brands are more acidic so experiment and find a brand you like. Honestly, imported tomatoes are usually sweeter and less acidic, but they are generally more expensive. The herbs, their age, and the exact amount you use will alter the taste, as will the meat.

If you want to tone down the acid taste, try adding more salt. Seriously, it works. You can add a pinch or two of sugar, but I don't like to do that. It seems like a counterfeit move to me. Add a few chunks of carrot and let them cook in the sauce then remove before serving. The sweetness of the carrot will help temper an acidic taste. Experiment with adding a few dashes of nutmeg or using a sweet wine for the liquid. If there was ever a time to be brave and experiment, this is the time to go fearless! If your sauce is ready and still seems too acidic to your taste, then go ahead and add a couple of pinches of sugar to taste. No one needs to know.

This recipe can be the base for many variations of sauce. Try using ground veal, pork, or Italian sausage as all or part of the meat component. If you choose chuck roast, cook low and long until the meat is tender and falls apart. Shred in large chunks and serve on top of the spaghetti. Making sauce with a piece of roast makes a delicious and rich sauce, unique in flavor, but it requires the longer cooking time to be sure the roast is tender. It's definitely worth the extra time and effort though.

Try adding black olives, green olives (1, not both), more garlic, red pepper flakes, or anchovy paste (reduce the salt if you do this). This sauce can be used to make many different dishes from spaghetti, lasagna, ravioli, to rigatoni. It is also delicious served over polenta. Be sure to have plenty of grated Reggiano and/or Parmesan cheese to serve on top and extra to pass at the table of your anxious, hungry eaters.

I hope you enjoy! Mangia bene!

—Gay G.

## Italian Meat Sauce

### *Ingredients*

1-1½ pound ground beef or 1½ pound chuck roast or use Italian sausage for all or part of the meat
1 medium onion chopped
4 cloves minced fresh garlic
2 Tablespoon chopped fresh basil (3 teaspoon dried)
3 teaspoon chopped fresh rosemary (2 teaspoon dried)
2 teaspoon fresh oregano (½ teaspoon dried)
1 large or 2 medium bay leaves
1 sprig fresh thyme (¼ teaspoon dried)

1-2 dashes dried red pepper flakes (optional)
1 cup chopped fresh mushrooms, or 4 ounces chopped dried Italian Porcinis (much, much better.)—Just chop them up or crush with your hands into small pieces and put into the sauce. Most stores have them; you may have to ask to find them.)
1 28-ounce can crushed tomatoes
1 cup white or red wine or beef broth (I never put plain water in sauce; it's a waste of time. Use a liquid that will add some flavor.) Add more liquid as it cooks down as needed for the consistency you like.
Note: Don't forget to add a carrot if you want to tone down the acidity of the tomatoes then remove before serving.

### *Directions*

In a heavy pot or Dutch oven, salt the meat and brown in olive oil over medium heat. While browning, chop onions, garlic, and herbs. When the meat is well browned, add the rest of the ingredients to the pot, stir well, cover, and simmer on low until meat is tender and the sauce has a lot of flavor. This can take up to 3 hours or more if you use the roast. You can also cook it in a crockpot but be sure to brown the meat in a hot pan first. Ground beef sauce should simmer at least 2 hours. Serve over your favorite pasta cooked al dente and top with grated Parmesan cheese. It's common to serve a bowl of extra sauce and bowl of cheese for your crew to add more to their own taste. This is enough sauce for approximately 1 lb. of pasta.
Make it your own: experiment with more or less of any of the ingredients until you are happy with it. Spaghetti sauce should be your own, though I have been trying to replicate my Aunt Sadie Ferrari's sauce my whole adult life and haven't quite mastered it yet!
Tip of the day: If you grow your own tomatoes, put a fish head at the base of each plant. I'm a terrible gardener, but this is what my uncle Roy Rosasco preached, and he grew fabulous tomatoes. My daughter, Allison, has tried it and says it works!

# SIDE-KICKIN' SIDES

# *FRENCH AU GRATIN POTATOES*

This is classic French cooking at its best. Simple, real ingredients that are so delicious. The potatoes, onions, and cheeses meld into a sublime creaminess. There is no white sauce, no cans of this or that. You will never want to return to the processed modern version after eating this elegant side dish. They are great for a holiday meal served alongside a prime rib, steaks, rack of lamb, roasted fowl, or other simple meat. I learned to use a mandolin for this recipe; both the onions and potatoes need to be that thin to bake into the luscious result. While this dish is certainly not on a diet menu, they are made with all whole, real foods. Don't try to use anything but real, heavy cream for this dish.

The number of potatoes and onions you need will be dependent upon the size of the dish you use, as will the amounts of the other ingredients. You will probably be surprised at how far a single potato and onion will go when sliced whisper-thin.

I love to use some Gruyere, along with Cheddars and Swiss, with Parmesan in this dish. The baking time will also vary dependent upon the type of potato and depth of the dish, I recommend at least a 3-inch-deep dish be used.

—Dea

Ingredients

3 to 4 russet potatoes
1 onion
Assorted grated cheeses such as Gruyere, Cheddars, and Parmesan
Heavy cream

### *Directions*

Grease a baking or casserole dish with butter
Place a layer of sliced very thinly sliced potatoes in the dish, and season with salt or garlic salt and pepper
Add a layer of sliced onion
Add a light layer of desired cheeses
Repeat layers a few times, ending with potato
Pour heavy cream over the layers, then press down the layers. The cream should cover or almost cover the layers
Sprinkle with desired cheese, I usually end with parmesan or asiago
Bake at 350 degrees for an hour to an hour and a half, the dish is done when poked with a fork or knife and is completely tender and the top is a lovely golden brown.
Let stand a few minutes before serving

## *TRIPLE B COWBOY BEANS*

We can't write a Cowboy Cuisine cookbook without including at least one classic cowboy-beans recipe. This is a "doozy"! It contains 3 different types of beans, all from cans. It's easy, easy, and will feed a crowd. Cooked in a slow cooker, you can make them, set the cooker on low, and when the party is ready so are your beans. That's the way we roll on cattle gathering day, brandings, and football games! Whatever your occasion, have fun feeding your crew! Remember, if the food is good, they'll come back next year. At this year's branding, my sister Kathy told one volunteer crew member (the best kind there is) that she was glad to see him again. He replied, "If the food is as good as it was last year, I'll always be back!" That's what we like to hear and that's the way we like to roll.

—Gay G.

Ingredients

1 pound ground chuck
1 pound bacon cut into small pieces
1 cup chopped onion
2 cans pork and beans
1 can kidney beans, drained
1 can butter/lima beans, drained
1 cup ketchup
½ cup brown sugar
1 Tablespoon liquid smoke
3 Tablespoon white vinegar
1 teaspoon salt
1 teaspoon black pepper

Directions

In large skillet fry bacon, drain off oil, and remove from pan. In same skillet, brown ground beef, drain off oil, and remove from skillet. In same pan, sauté onions until tender. Combine all ingredients in a slow cooker and stir well. Cover and cook on low 4-5 hours. Enjoy your cowboy beans.

Serves a crowd or a crew!

# *SOUTHWEST RANCH BEANS*

Here's another bean recipe. This is one of my husband's favorites. We grew up eating beans, a big variety of beans. From Butter beans to Pintos and everything in between. Besides enjoying the different kinds of beans, my family had many methods of seasoning them. Beans have always been a ranch staple, either in their dried form sitting on the shelf or waiting in a can. They can be a meal when cooked with a ham or bacon, or they can be served alongside a meat as a side dish. I've always loved their versatility.

I always try to have a ham hock, bacon ends, or the bone and trimmings from a ham leftover in the freezer. They lend such great flavor to beans.

I learned as a young wife and mother about altitude and cooking when we moved to a ranch in Northeastern Nevada. Beans don't cook in an hour or two when you're above 6,000 feet elevation. You will need to adjust the cooking time to fit your altitude.

You can serve this version of pintos alongside almost anything, including Mexican food.

—Dea

## *Ingredients*

2 cups of rinsed, dried pinto beans
1 ham hock or a ham bone
¼ cup chopped bacon ends
Water
1 small onion chopped
3 Tablespoon minced garlic
1 Tablespoon Worcestershire Sauce
1 teaspoon liquid smoke flavoring
1 Tablespoon red chile powder
½ cup diced jalapeno peppers
2 Tablespoon brown sugar
Salt and black pepper

## *Directions*

Rinse and then soak beans in water overnight.
Drain beans and place in a pot with 6 cups of water. Add all other ingredients. You can cook on top of the stove or put in a crockpot for several hours. When the beans are almost done, remove the ham bone, and allow to cool a few minutes. When you can handle the meat dice it and return to pot. Adjust the seasoning and serve. Canned tomatoes can be added, making these into a variation of Charro beans.

# *SHEEPHERDER'S BREAD*

I learned to make this easy bread from my neighbors while living on a very remote ranch in northeastern Nevada. I made it every other day for decades. I had 6 to 7 people to feed every day at least, with the closest grocery store over an hour away, in good weather.

The flours can be changed, as long as you start with 4 cups of white all-purpose for the base. Whole wheat and other flours can be used for the additional flour, as well as oatmeal, cornmeal, cracked wheat, etc. for variety. You can also replace part of the sugar with honey, and eggs can be added for more nutrition. I baked this in two large loaf pans or a two 9-inch cake pans, rather than as one large loaf in a Dutch oven. This also makes great dinner rolls. It is similar to a soft French bread. This recipe works very well at high altitude, too.

—Dea

## *Ingredients*

½ cup butter
½ cup white sugar
2 teaspoon salt
3 cups very hot water
2 packages of yeast (4 teaspoon)
7 to 8 cups of flour

Directions

In a large bowl place butter (chopped if cold), sugar, and salt. Add the hot water, stir 'til butter is melted and the mixture is just warm, about 115 degrees. Test on your wrist to ensure it isn't too hot, It should feel lukewarm. Stir in yeast, let the yeast sit 'til bubbly, about 15 minutes. Add 4 cups of the white all-purpose flour; beat well. Gradually add in around 3 to 4 more cups flour; this will depend on which flours you are using. Turn onto a floured board and knead until smooth, about 5 to 10 minutes. Return dough to bowl, cover with a cloth, and place in a warm place until doubled. Punch down and place on a floured board, cut dough in half. Use one half at a time, roll, and shape to fit a greased pan, making sure all edges are sealed. Repeat with the other half. Let the shaped dough rise 'til double again.
Bake at 375 degrees around 45 minutes 'til golden brown. Check for doneness- loaf sounds hollow when removed from the pan and gently knocked or tapped on the bottom. Remove from pan and allow to cool by placing bread on racks, or by placing the loaves across the loaf pan.
For dinner rolls, pat or roll dough out into two rectangles. Using a sharp knife cut into squares, equal in size. Roll each square into a ball, placing the sealed edge bottom down in the pan. Let rise again until doubled and bake at 375 degrees for about 20 to 25 minutes.

## *GARLIC CARROTS*

If you are one of those people who doesn't like the sweet sugary carrot dishes so common in your grandmother's kitchen (verging on blasphemy, we understand), this may be just the carrot recipe you've been looking for, and it couldn't be easier! Grandma was right when she told you to eat carrots because they were good for your eyesight. (Or was that Bugs Bunny?) Anyway, carrots are full of Beta carotene, the precursor to Vitamin A, and really are good for your eyesight. They're also darn good, full of nutrition, and add beautiful color to the dinner plate! That's what's up, Doc!

—Gay G.

Ingredients

1 small package baby carrots
⅓ – ½ cup olive oil
2-3 cloves fresh garlic, peeled and minced fine
2 Tablespoon fresh chopped parsley

Directions

Rinse and drain carrots, cut into ½ inch pieces. Steam or microwave until just tender but not mushy. While carrots are steaming, melt butter over medium-low heat; add minced garlic and sauté for 3-4 minutes. It's important to use low heat so garlic and butter don't burn. When carrots are done, drain any liquid and add to butter/garlic mixture. Add chopped parsley and stir well to coat carrots. That's it; simple, pretty, and tasty!

Serves 4

## *MARINATED WHITE BEAN SALAD*

This is a delightful cold salad that compliments beef, pork, chicken, or lamb. Make it ahead and keep chilled in refrigerator. Take it out and bring to room temperature before ready to serve (about 1 hour). This also makes a great dish on a buffet or appetizer table and travels well for picnics and potlucks.

—Gay G.

### *Ingredients*

1 pound of dry small white beans or cannellini beans
1 bunch of green onions chopped, include green part
1½ teaspoon salt
1½ teaspoon pepper
½ teaspoon celery salt
2 cloves finely minced garlic (or 1 teaspoon garlic powder)
2 Tablespoon fresh chopped parsley (more if you like)
1 cup olive oil
1 cup white vinegar
¼ cup water

### *Directions*

Cook beans uncovered in simmering water, adding water as needed, until tender. You can cook them in a crockpot on high, so you don't have to watch them as carefully. Will take about 3 hrs. to be done or cook on low overnight. Be sure to cover beans in the crockpot with at least 2 inches of water over them.
When done, rinse beans carefully and drain well. Cool. In a bowl, combine beans and all other ingredients. Mix well. These are best made ahead of time and allowed to marinate for several hours or overnight before serving.
Make it Easy
Substitute 5 cans of white or cannellini beans, rinsed well, for the dry beans. Takes only a few minutes to put this together and people will think you've worked all day. Be sure to bow when they applaud.

# *REAL DEAL MAC & CHEESE*

Macaroni and cheese has been a favorite dish in the USA since Thomas Jefferson is reported to have brought back macaroni from Europe. We've all used the famous boxed variety, sometimes adding ingredients to it to make it better. It is a dish that can be kid-pleasing or sophisticated enough for an adult's taste. The recipe below is basic and one without flour or the usual pasty thickener; it is all about being creamy and cheesy.

Green chiles, jalapenos, and bacon can be added to really kick the flavors up. If you use bacon, remember to cut back on the salt. The flavors and varieties of cheeses can be changed for personal taste, too. Swiss, Gruyere, and other great melting cheeses are wonderful with the cheddar.

—Dea

## *Ingredients*

8 ounce dry macaroni (about 2 scant cups)
2 cups of heavy cream
½ cup of sharp Cheddar
½ cup of Monterey Jack
1 cup of additional cheese

## *Directions*

Preheat oven to very hot, about 500 degrees
Boil the dry macaroni, drain and set aside
Place the heavy cream in a large pot
When it begins to get hot, but not boil
Add:
Sharp Cheddar
Monterey Jack
Stir until cheeses are melted
Remove from heat and stir in the cooked macaroni
Sprinkle black pepper over mixture
Place mixture in a greased casserole dish
Top with 1 cup of cheese; I mix Parmesan and Cheddar, or even Asiago. A layer of bread or Panko crumbs with butter drizzled over them can be added, too
Bake 'til crust is golden brown, it won't take long, so watch it. Let stand a few minutes before serving

You won't ever want to go back to the box after eating this.

## *ZUCCHINI CASSEROLE*

This is a variation of my Aunt Sadie Dickinson's recipe. She was a wonderful lady and an extraordinary cook. She lived in Fresno, Ca. area and used roasted and peeled canned Ortega peppers. When she and my Uncle Al would come up to visit, we'd have large family barbeques, and this is one of the delicious dishes Sadie would make. I've used freshly roasted, frozen, or canned green chile peppers. You don't need to worry about the brand name of the green chiles; they're all fine for this. You can also mix the cheeses to your preference, using Jack, Cheddar, Swiss, Parm, etc. or any combination of them. This recipe can easily be cut in half, and yellow summer squash or calabacita squash can be used.

—Dea

### Ingredients

2 small cans of roasted and peeled whole green chiles or the equivalent amount of frozen or fresh green chiles
4 or 5 medium zucchini or other summer squash sliced into thin rounds
2 cups of grated cheese

Garlic salt
3 beaten eggs
¾ cup biscuit/baking mix
1¼ cup of milk
Black pepper
½ teaspoon oregano
Sea salt

### *Directions*

Preheat oven to 350 degrees. Grease a 13 x 9 inch glass dish. Split the peppers, remove any seeds, and make a layer of them to roughly cover the bottom of the dish. Next, place a layer of the squash; it is okay to overlap the slices. Sprinkle with garlic salt, then sprinkle with 1 cup of the cheese. In a bowl beat the eggs slightly, add the biscuit/baking mix, milk, and seasonings, mix well. Pour half the mixture over the layers. Repeat the layers, finishing with the rest of the liquid mixture. Sprinkle additional cheese on top if desired.
Bake for about an hour, until top is golden brown, and squash are tender. Let stand a few minutes before serving.

## SHARON'S RICE PILAF

My dear friend Sharon made this pilaf for a dinner party many years ago. It was so memorable; I called her the next morning begging her to share the recipe with me. She's a good friend, let's make that a great friend, and she graciously shared the recipe. It pairs so well with the Teriyaki Flank Steak recipe included in this book that I have reserved it for dinners when flank is on the menu, but it is equally delicious as a side for chicken or fish. If serving it with fish or fowl, substitute chicken broth for the beef broth for a lighter taste.

To my recollection, I don't think I've ever made a single recipe of this pilaf. I always double it to be sure there is enough for everyone to have seconds because they usually do. And there will be enough for leftovers the next day.

—Gay G.

### Ingredients

5 Tablespoon butter
2 coils fideo pasta
1 cup long-grain rice
1 can beef broth
¼ teaspoon garlic powder
1 cup sliced mushrooms (optional)

### Directions

Melt 2 Tablespoon butter in a sauté pan over medium heat. Add rice and fideo pasta (break it up into small pieces) and brown. In a sauté pan with lid, combine beef broth, ½ can water, garlic powder, remaining 3 Tablespoon. butter, and mushrooms. Bring to gentle boil then pour into rice/fideo pan. Cover and simmer 25 minutes. Add more liquid if needed. Salt and pepper to taste. Serves 4

# *CALABACITAS*

The recipe below is a variation of the historic New Mexican Calabacitas recipe. The story is that in the late Fall baby pumpkins that would not have time to mature were used in this very old recipe, hence the name in Spanish for baby pumpkins or squash. Historically a dish of late Summer or early Fall, it is based on the famous New Mexico crops of green chile, summer squash, onion, and corn. I often make this dish without the corn, sometimes add tomatoes and even sweet, red, and yellow peppers. Any summer squash will work, including yellow, patty pan, zucchini, and the calabacita or Mexican squash. It makes a bright, flavorful dish and you can add ingredients as you like. Below is my easy basic version of this dish we enjoy frequently with a variety of main dishes/meats.

—Dea

## *Ingredients*

2 Tablespoon oil
Garlic salt
Black pepper
2 calabacita type squash or other summer squash, sliced or cut into small cubes
¼ cup diced onion
½ cup of corn
3 roasted, diced green chiles
½ cup cherry tomatoes (optional)
Shredded cheese of choice; Cheddars, Asiago, and Jack are all good choices

## *Directions*

Heat oil in a large skillet
Sauté onion until it begins to soften
Add the rest of the veggies, sprinkling with garlic salt liberally
Lift and stir the veggies, cooking to desired doneness
Add more garlic salt and sprinkle with black pepper
Top with shredded cheese and enjoy

Recipe can easily be doubled or tripled

## *SHORTCUT AU GRATIN SPUDS*

Everyone has a story about their first job and I'm no exception. Some of my friends in high school worked as aides at the hospital during summer vacation. Some were those cute carhops on roller skates. Then there were those of us who worked in the potato sheds grading potatoes. It was a great job.

My dear friend, Pam, and I had a great time working in the sheds. Our workday often started at 6:00 a.m. and sometimes would go until midnight. It didn't take us long to realize the benefits of "time and a half" for overtime. At a minimum hourly rate then of $1.50/hr. it meant we'd earn $2.25/hr. for everything over 8 hours of work. Holy Cow…that was big money for High School kids in those days! We were the graders, sorting the cull potatoes off the line as they came in from the water baths after the trucks dumped them. The guys were the sack sowers (jiggers) and truckers who trucked the boxes and sacks into the semi-trucks and rail cars. They were earning piece-work wages, so I think they probably made more than we did but jigging and trucking was hard work, so it was okay. They sure earned it.

Katy Rohrbach ran our crew, and she was in her 80s then. I guess you'd say she was a professional potato grader! Katy was a sweetheart, but she took her job seriously and you better be on the line in your place when the buzzer rang. One didn't mess with Katy! She was the kind of boss every young person should be so lucky to have. Our hour was 55 minutes of the belt running and then a 5-minute break. A loud BUZZZZ would ring and it all started again. You had barely enough time to hit the Ladies' Room fast and get back to it. Some of the older women were smokers and they had to hit the room AND get in a few cigarette puffs before the buzzer went off again. I always marveled at their attention to that addiction; they were dedicated smokers for sure. Pam and I, the youngsters on the crew, had no interest in smoking. We used our precious extra 1.5 minutes to visit with Greg and his cute buddy. BUZZZZ, and it was back to the "office". Potatoes were rolling and there was no time to waste.

You might think we would have sworn off eating potatoes after watching 2 million of them roll past, but that's not the case. I love potatoes and I love the memories of those summer days. It's where I learned what it meant to really work. In the beginning, all we wanted was for the trucks to quit coming from the field. That would mean they'd quit digging potatoes and we could go home. If I looked out and saw six trucks lined up and it was already 4:00 p.m., my heart sank. But somewhere along the way that summer, it clicked. I realized the value of a real job, the value of work. It was a growing up experience and I've been thankful for it all my life. As a college professor, I've often told the story just to let students know I started at the bottom of the ladder, too, and that the lessons I learned there were some of the most important ones of my life. I'm proud that I was once a "spud grader".

Pam went on to become Dr. Pam, Ph.D. One day she was in town visiting her wonderful parents. (I loved Mr. and Mrs. Stennes.) She and I were sitting at their kitchen table having coffee when Mr. S. came in from tending his orange trees. As he walked by us, we heard him say, "Not bad for two potato shed workers." I guess he had worried about us, or at least me, when we were young. Well, we'd made it and he was proud. It meant a lot.

Today, when you open a bag of potatoes and find one that's rotten or badly misshapen or scarred, think of Katy Rohrbach. That would never happen on Katy's watch!

—Gay G

## Ingredients

1 large package frozen shredded hash browns or country potatoes (your choice). If you prefer fresh potatoes, use 5 peeled Russet potatoes that have been baked until tender, cooled and shredded or cubed (Your choice again, so many choices)
1 can cream of celery or chicken soup (more choices to make, this makes cooking fun!)
½ can milk
1 cup sour cream
2 cups grated cheddar cheese (Do you like medium or sharp? Your choice, but don't use mild cheddar, there just isn't enough flavor for this dish.)

## Directions

In a saucepan, combine soup, milk, sour cream, and cheese. Heat over medium-low heat until cheese has completely melted. Season with black pepper and stir well. In a large mixing bowl, combine slightly thawed potatoes and soup mixture. Stir well. Pour into greased 9x13 baking dish.
Cover and bake at 350 degrees for 30 minutes. Uncover and bake an addition 15 minutes or until lightly browned.

Serves 6-8

# *DANDY DESSERTS*

# *BERRY SOPAPILLA CHEESECAKE*

I love sopapilla cheesecake. If you've ever had sopapillas, you'll love it, too. When I was a kid, the fried sopapillas were often served with strawberry jam. A teaspoon or two of the jam was spooned into the hollow pocket of the sopapilla. In many places in the Southwest, they are sprinkled with cinnamon sugar, and then honey is poured on them or in them, and there's no jam. So, the first time I had sopapilla cheesecake, it was like the sopapillas they serve with the honey, but, better and with a great creamy richness. It made me think about how much better it would be with the little tart contrast of fruit. So, I came up with this recipe. It is one of my fast and easy recipes that uses a store-bought, processed product because everyone needs a little break once in a while. And it is so good, you won't mind.

The biscuits that came in a can or tube earned the name of whomp biscuits when I was a kid, because you "whomped" them on the edge of the counter or table to get them to pop open. Nowadays, you are supposed to put a spoon in the seam to get them open. I still jump when they actually pop open.

—Dea

## *Ingredients*

1 roll or tube of crescent rolls (found by the whomp biscuits in the refrigerator section in the store)
1 8 ounce package of cream cheese brought to room temperature
1 egg
Scant ½ cup of sugar
1 teaspoon vanilla
½ cup fresh or frozen berries (I love using raspberries)
½ cup melted butter
½ teaspoon cinnamon
¼ cup sugar
Honey

## *Directions*

Preheat oven to 350 degrees
Spray an 8 or 9-inch square baking pan. Open the crescent rolls and gently unroll them out on a board. Take ½ of the pieces and patch back together if necessary, then roll them lightly to the size to cover the bottom of the baking pan, an 8 or 9-inch square. Place this in the baking dish for a bottom crust.
Beat the cream cheese until smooth, gradually add in the ½ cup of sugar, then beat in the egg and the vanilla 'til mixture is smooth and creamy.
Spread the cream cheese mixture over the rolled crust in the pan. Sprinkle on the berries.

Roll the remaining half of the dough into a square like the first half. Place this over the fruit and cream cheese filling. Mix the melted butter, remaining sugar, and cinnamon in a small bowl. Spread this over the top of the rolled crust

Bake about 30 minutes, 'til puffed and golden brown.

If desired, honey can be drizzled on the top as soon as the cheesecake comes out of the oven. Cool before slicing. This recipe can easily be doubled, you will use a 13 x 9-inch pan. Blackberries, blueberries, strawberries, and even cherries are delicious to use in this recipe.

## *COWBOY COCONUT CREAM PIE*

This is a stepped-up version of a classic cream pie, made from scratch. Folks who don't like coconut might want to try this one. The love of coconut pies or any dessert with coconut goes back to the days when it was a luxury and considered exotic in the West, much like pineapple. These things were hard to come by, especially on ranches.

This pie has the addition of both toasted coconut and toasted almonds on the top, with coconut in a vanilla custard for the filling. You might want to even forgo the whipped cream with this pie.

I use a wire whisk when making cream pies, from mixing the dry ingredients to the last step of cooking the custard to ensure a velvety texture.

This recipe for the basic pie crust is one I've used ever since I was a kid. A tender, flaky crust makes all the difference when making pies.

—Dea

## *Filling Ingredients*

2 or 3 eggs, beaten
⅔ cup sugar
½ teaspoon salt
1 Tablespoon flour
2½ Tablespoon cornstarch
3 cups of milk
½ cup of flaked coconut
2 Tablespoon butter
2 teaspoon vanilla

## *Topping Ingredients*

1 Tablespoon butter
¼ cup of slivered almonds
½ cup flaked coconut

## *Directions*

Make a single crust pie shell and have it cool and ready. In small bowl beat eggs 'til lemon colored, set aside. In a saucepan, mix the sugar, salt, corn starch, and flour. Gradually add in milk, whisk well. Bring barely to a boil and then remove from heat. Pour and stir a small amount of the mixture into the eggs.
Place the saucepan back on low heat and add the egg mixture, stirring constantly. Allow it to thicken, a minute or two is all that's required, don't raise the heat or stop stirring or you will have pieces of egg in the custard. When thickened, immediately remove from heat and add ½ cup coconut, 2 Tablespoon butter, and 2 tsp vanilla, whisk until smooth. Pour the custard into the prepared pie shell. Set aside, chill if you have time.

## *Before serving:*

In a small skillet place 1 Tablespoon butter, add ½ cup each of coconut and slivered almonds. Cook on med/low heat for a few minutes, stirring often. Cook just 'til the coconut is golden brown, being careful to not overcook and burn the coconut. Let the topping cool and sprinkle it on the cooled pie before serving.
A dollop of whip cream can be used on each slice if desired, though this pie is fairly rich.

# *TRIED & TRUE PIE CRUST*

I've always made pies. Cream pies, fruit pies, nut pies, even meat pies. Pies and cobblers were preferred over cakes for dessert on the ranch I grew up on, although my Granddad "built" some awfully good cakes. When folks neighbored (helped each other with cattle works) or attended an event, the ranch brand of the pie maker was cut into the pie crust, acting as vents. It was a way to show which ranch cook made that particular pie. Of course, the cook was also proud of their efforts and it didn't hurt for folks to know who brought which pie.

When we were first married I made pies at home and delivered them to various restaurants. It was something I could do at home to earn money without paying for a babysitter. This is the pie crust I've always used; simple, and always flaky and perfect. I've tried various recipes over the years and this is my favorite. You can use store-bought crust, but it just isn't the same.

I've heard folks say they can't make pie crust, I think it is all in the cutting in of the shortening or lard. Use a pastry blender, one of the half-circle, hand-held ones. I used to use 2 butter knives before I knew they made pasty blenders. I really think you will get the hang of it if you do it a few times. It is worth the effort. Another thing for the inexperienced baker to know is that if your crust wants to fall apart and is somewhat difficult to handle, it is probably going to be really good. Just patch it together and go on. If someone wants a perfect looking pie, they can go buy one. It won't compare in taste to the one you make, though.

—Dea

## *Ingredients*

For 1 single crust:
1½ cups of flour
½ teaspoon salt
½ cup shortening or lard
4 to 5 Tablespoon cold water

For double crust:
2 cups of flour
1 teaspoon salt
⅔ cup of shortening or lard
5 to 7 Tablespoon of cold water

## *Directions*

Using a fork, stir flour, and salt together in a medium size or larger bowl. Cut in most of the lard or shortening using a pastry blender until it is really cut in, resembling a coarse meal, and leaving a few lumps smaller than small peas. Sprinkle about ⅓ of the water over the dough, fluff and turn the dough with the fork gently, repeat twice, until all the dough is moistened.
Grab a good-sized handful and form into a ball, about the size of a softball. Place on a floured surface and sprinkle a little more flour on the dough. Using a rolling pin start rolling the dough from the center, change and go the opposite way, from the center. Roll until the desired size is achieved. Gently place the rolling

pen near the edge of dough. Using a small flat spatula or butter knife, slide it under the dough and lift the dough, placing it around the rolling pin until the dough is loosely wrapped around the pin and can be picked up and unrolled over the pie pan. You can also use a floured silicone sheet to roll the dough on, and then place the pie pan upside down on it. Flip the sheet and pie pan upright and peel the silicone sheet off the dough directly into the pan.

Crimp the edges using your finger and thumb or simply mash down the edge with a fork. You can get fancy with the crust, but another easy decoration for the rim is to push a measuring teaspoon against the side, making a pretty scallop. Prick the bottom in a few places.

Bake an unfilled single-crust at 450 degrees for 10 to 15 minutes.

# *14 CARAT CAKE*

This fabulous carrot cake recipe is a crowd favorite. It's easy to make, and unlike some cakes, this one comes out the same every time. Great for big gatherings, it's rich and filling so a 9X13 cake will go a long way. It can also be baked in three 9" round pans to make a tall, beautiful layer cake. Don't overlook all the health benefits, too, like better vision and appetites, right? Gotta "spin" the carrot thing, don't you? As cakes go, this really is a 14-carat diamond version. If you cook for compliments, as my friend Leanne proclaims, this one will bring 'em on!

—Gay G.

## *Ingredients*

2 cups all-purpose flour
2 teaspoon baking powder
1½ teaspoon baking soda
2 teaspoon cinnamon
1 teaspoon salt
2 cups sugar
1½ cup vegetable oil
1 teaspoon vanilla
4 eggs
2 cups grated carrots (lightly packed in measuring cup)
12 ounce drained can crushed pineapple
½ cup chopped walnuts or pecans

## *Directions*

Sift or whisk together flour, baking powder, baking soda, salt, and cinnamon. Add sugar, oil, and eggs and mix well. Stir in carrots, nuts, and pineapple. Turn into greased and floured 9X13 pan or 3 greased, floured and parchment paper-lined round baking cake pans. Bake at 350 degrees for 50-55 minutes (less for round pans). Cake is done when toothpick comes out clean. Be sure to test and not over bake.

## *Cream Cheese Frosting*

½ cup soft butter
1 8 ounce package Cream Cheese softened at room temperature
1 pound powdered sugar
½ cup chopped pecans or walnuts

Beat ingredients together and add ½ cup chopped pecans or walnuts. Frost cooled cake. For something a little different, the Rum Sauce Topping below is also quite delish and makes for a fancier dessert. Everyone loves a bit of fancy now and then, even the guys do when it tastes as good as this cake.

## *Rum Sauce Topping*

1 cup sugar
½ cup melted butter
3 Tablespoon flour
½ cup boiling water
1 teaspoon ground nutmeg
2 Tablespoon rum
1-2 Tablespoon heavy cream (optional)

Mix flour and sugar add to melted butter. Add ½ cup boiling water, nutmeg, and rum. You can add a little cream to this sauce at the end, if you like. I do.

# *BURGUNDY CHERRY ICE CREAM*

A few years ago, a company came out with an ice cream maker that doesn't require keeping salt or ice on hand. I bought two of them and love them. For someone who lives a long way to a store, or someone who doesn't care to continually run to the store, it was the answer to prayers. When I was a kid, homemade ice cream was truly a labor of love, kids laboring to make what they loved! My sisters and I took turns churning and sitting on the old wooden ice cream churn that was covered with a quilt for added insulation.

I am fortunate to have a big, old, wonderful sweet cherry tree, along with a more tart type cherry tree. We make lots of cherry desserts and this ice cream is a favorite, right next to cherry pie. I do prefer to use the sweeter cherry in this, or I mix the tart and sweet cherries for this ice cream.

While this ice cream has always been called Burgundy cherry, there is no burgundy wine in it. I use a merlot, a pinot noir, or even occasionally a chardonnay. The alcohol is "cooked out" of this recipe, so it is great for kids, as well. The addition of a dark chocolate garnish or accompaniment takes it to an adult level.

—Dea

### *Ingredients for the cherries*

1 pound of pitted halved or chopped cherries
2 Tablespoon honey
2 Tablespoon sugar
1 teaspoon cinnamon
½ cup of wine

### *Ingredients for ice cream*

1 egg
¾ cup of sugar
1 teaspoon vanilla
2 cups of heavy cream
1 cup of milk

### *Directions for cherries*

In a saucepan place about ½ the cherries, honey, sugar, cinnamon, and wine. Mix well and bring to a boil. Lower heat and cook gently a few minutes until reduced a bit. Remove the cherries from the liquid and cool separately. Meanwhile, make the ice cream.

## *Directions for ice cream*

Beat egg, add sugar and vanilla. Add milk and heavy cream. Whisk 'til thoroughly blended. Add in up to 1/2 cup of the reserved syrup, whisk thoroughly. Cover and return to refrigerator for a few hours or overnight. Churn ice cream according to your machine; add the cold, reserved cherries the last five minutes either by hand or machine. Freeze.

To serve, place scoops in pretty ice cream dishes and garnish with dark chocolate shavings. A small piece of the chocolate, or some grated pieces work well, or simply stand a dark chocolate cookie, like an Oreo, alongside the scoop. This is grown-up ice cream at its best.

## FRONTIER CHEESECAKE

This cheesecake is so easy to make and rivals the best cheesecake you'll find in New York or any fine restaurant. According to historians, cheesecake dates to the early Greeks and was a favorite of brides to serve at their wedding. It may also have been served to athletes in the first Olympics to give them energy. Cheesecake…the dessert of the ages. You'll be making history with this one!

—Gay G.

## Crust Ingredients

1 box vanilla wafers
6 Tablespoon melted butter
½ cup nuts chopped fine

## Directions

Cut a round of parchment paper to fit the bottom of an 8-inch or 9inch greased springform pan (depending on how thick you want your cake) and put in place. Mix all ingredients and press into springform pan, coming up edges about 1 inch.
Bake at 300 degrees for 10 minutes (You can make Graham Cracker crust if you prefer.)

## Filling Ingredients

3 cartons softened Philadelphia Cream Cheese
1 cup sugar
2 Tablespoon clear vanilla
2 eggs

## Directions

Mix cream cheese smooth in a food processor or mixing bowl with an electric mixer. Add other ingredients and mix thoroughly. Pour into vanilla wafer crust and bake at 300 degrees for 50-60 minutes. Cheesecake is done when a knife inserted in center comes out clean.
Cool then cover with plastic wrap and chill in springform pan several hours or overnight before serving. To serve, remove pan ring and plate on a flat cake plate or serving plate.
Serve alone or with raspberry, strawberry, or chocolate sauce, or be creative. Garnish with fresh fruit and sweet whipped cream (optional).

## *FLOURLESS CHOCOLATE CAKE*

Flourless cake recipes have been around for a long time, but my experience with them hasn't been so good until this recipe came along. It has actually become one of my favorites because many people want to eat less processed flour these days. Or at least pretend to.

This cake is dark, rich, and stays moist for days if you keep it covered. Similar in texture to a brownie, it's delicious frosted with buttercream or chocolate frosting. Add some nuts to the frosting if you like. Don't be afraid to serve it to guests, especially your gluten intolerant ones. Top with cherry pie filling and whipped cream for a mock Black Forest dessert. Your fans will thank you.

—Gay G.

## *Ingredients*

¾ cup butter
12 ounce bittersweet chocolate (use the best quality chocolate you can find)
6 eggs
1¼ cup granulated sugar
½ teaspoon salt (preferably kosher salt)
1 teaspoon vanilla extract

## *Directions*

Preheat oven to 325 degrees. Generously butter bottom and sides of one 9-inch x 2-inch deep round cake pan. Dust with flour. Line bottom of the pan with parchment paper, smoothing to eliminate air bubbles. Parchment paper is the best invention since the wheel. You'll always want to use it when baking cakes to guarantee they don't stick to the pan.

Coarsely chop 12 oz good-quality bittersweet chocolate into ½-inch pieces and put in a medium saucepan. Add butter to saucepan and cook over low heat, stirring occasionally with a heatproof spatula, until butter and chocolate are melted. Don't rush. It will take several minutes if heat is on low enough. Remove pan from heat and let cool to room temperature, about 15 minutes. (You can encourage the chocolate mixture to cool faster by occasionally stirring it and/or set in refrigerator for a couple of minutes only.)

Meanwhile, using an electric mixer on high speed, beat 6 large eggs, 1¼ cups granulated sugar, 1/2 tsp kosher salt, and 1 tsp vanilla in a large bowl. Beat until pale yellow and fluffy, 8–11 minutes. This is a very important step in making the flourless cake. It's ready when the egg mixture has almost tripled in volume, the beaters start to create a ribboning effect, and when you lift the beaters, the mixture should leave a trail as it falls back on itself.

Pour in the cooled chocolate mixture. Gently fold together with a rubber spatula by scooping underneath, then cutting through the middle with the side of the spatula. Continue folding just until batter is well combined. It's important not to over mix or you'll lose the fluffiness of the eggs.

Pour mixture into prepared 9-inch round cake pan and bake on middle rack at 325 degrees for approximately 30 minutes. Altitude always affects how a cake bakes and since this is flourless, there is no altitude adjustment except for the baking time. Test with a toothpick. Cake is done when it comes out clean.

## *DRUNKEN FRUIT, TUTTI-FRUITY, AND A HOT TODDY RECIPES*

### *Tutti-Fruity*

When I was a kid, my Granddad would salvage older summer fruit, you know the kind, starting to be not-so-fresh, but you don't want to waste it. Especially when viewed by someone who had gone through the Great Depression. Anyway, he'd place the fruit, a layer of sugar, and a small amount of whiskey in a crock, or some glass or ceramic container he could cover. The addition of the whiskey helped speed up the fermentation. Some folks might use vodka or gin, etc.

He'd add on to this as the fruit became available, layering more fruit and sugar, (don't add any more alcohol) and letting it ferment. Almost every kind of fruit was used, melons, berries, peaches, and apples. Around the holidays, he would declare it was ready to be eaten. He always called it Tutti- Fruity and it was served over cake or ice cream as a special treat. We kids got a very small amount on our ice cream or cake.

### *Burgundy Cherry*

We'd go see my city cousins once a year or so. I discovered a flavor of ice cream in the city that was somewhat hard to come by where we lived. I had forgotten about it until I heard someone mention Burgundy Cherry ice cream, and those memories of that delicious creamy, palest-of-pink ice cream studded with rich red cherries came flooding back. I am sure the ice cream I had as a kid didn't have any wine, even if the alcohol was all cooked out. So, I did some research and came up with the recipe I've included in this book.

### *Drunken Fruit*

But while we are on the subject, let me tell you what else I discovered. Drunken berries, or drunken fruit. The folks in my bunch all enjoy a nice glass of wine, usually of the red, dry varieties. Even if you aren't a wine lover, you will likely love this recipe. Here are the basics of this yummy recipe for drunken fruit. Berries and cherries work best. Simply take your desired fruit and place in a saucepan, sprinkle some sugar with cinnamon in it onto the fruit. Feel free to experiment and add some herbs like basil or mint. You don't want a lot of sugar, just enough to take the pucker factor out. Place the fruit and herbs if you are using them, into a saucepan. Pour enough wine in to cover the bottom of the pan. Add an almost equal amount of water. Let the fruit gently poach until the sauce is reduced and thickened. It should only take a few minutes. Use the fruit warm or store in the fridge. You can also use sliced apples, peaches, etc., and use bourbon or another liquor in place of the wine. As an example, a great combination is diced peaches, bourbon, brown sugar, and cinnamon. Raspberries, merlot, and basil are great combinations, too.

The fruit and sauce is wonderful over ice cream, pound or angel food cakes, cheesecakes, bread pudding, custards, whatever you think will make a great dessert even better. If you use larger fruits, dice them into berry size bites.

## *Favorite Toddy*

I sometimes have issues sleeping, and if it is a cold night, I really want to be able to relax. A favorite toddy I enjoy is the following. It isn't calorie conscience, but, it is warming and yummy and I sure sleep better after a mug of this.

In a coffee mug, make about ½ to ⅔ cup of hot cocoa. I use the instant mix I keep on hand for grandkids and other young visitors. Get it good and hot. Add a good dose of Irish Cream Liquor like Baileys or Carolans; you can use either the regular or the caramel flavored. Top with a squirt of whipped cream or a scoop of ice cream. I also drizzle with either chocolate or caramel syrup if I feel like I really need the extra comfort after a long day working in the cold. Cuddle up in front of the fire, in a warm blanket or afghan and enjoy, this is real comfort food!

—Dea

## NANNER PUDDIN'

We all have those childhood memories of food. Maybe they were special because of who made them, or maybe they were only made at special times. One of those memories for me is what our family called Nanner Puddin'. It was always topped with meringue, or calf slobbers, as my Grandad called it. I am not talking about boxes of instant pudding mix layered with bananas and cookies and finished with artificial topping. This is the real deal, just like my Granny made it. I remember the old red handled rotary egg beaters she used for the meringue, and getting to take a turn whirring them through the egg whites while she sprinkled sugar on the egg whites. There are just some old things and some old recipes you don't mess with. This is one.

—Dea

Preheat oven to 450 degrees

## Ingredients

1 to 2 ripe bananas
½ box of Vanilla wafer cookies
3 eggs
⅔ cup sugar
½ teaspoon salt
2½ Tablespoon cornstarch
1 Tablespoon flour
3 cups of whole milk
2 Tablespoon butter
1 teaspoon vanilla

## Directions

In a small bowl place 3 yolks and whisk 'til broken, place the 3 whites in a larger bowl, set both aside.

In a saucepan mix the sugar, salt, cornstarch, and flour, gradually whisk in milk 'til smooth. Place on stove on medium heat and bring to a boil while stirring, then turn heat to low. Add a small amount of the hot liquid to the yolks, stirring to mix. Pour the mixture into the saucepan and stir, while bringing to a boil, then boil 1 minute or until thickened. Remove from heat and add butter and vanilla.

Layer an oven-proof bowl with vanilla wafer cookies, then layer banana slices over the cookies. Then add a layer of the custard, repeat the layers of cookies, and sliced bananas until the custard is all used and it is the top layer.

Beat the egg whites until soft peaks form, sprinkle in 1 Tablespoon sugar gradually while beating the meringue. Continue beating the egg whites until stiff peaks form, and all sugar is totally dissolved. Pile meringue on the warm pudding, making sure to seal the edges and the entire surface is covered. Using a spoon, pull up the meringue into pretty peaks. Bake the pudding 'til the meringue is golden brown, usually 5 to 10 minutes. Let cool before serving. Refrigerate any leftovers.

## *GAUCHO CHOCOLATE TRUFFLES*

Almost everyone likes something sweet and chocolaty. These gems are so easy to make and are the stuff royalty might dine on after a feast. Your meals are feasts and you are royalty, so why not serve up some of these delicious jewels to finish off dinner. They're also great to make for holidays and dessert buffets. Make them ahead of time and store in the refrigerator until ready to serve. They'll travel well, too, just don't let them get hot. You know, chocolate melts and these will melt in your hand, not in your mouth!

—Gay G

### *Ingredients*

12 ounce good-quality Bakers Chocolate (unsweetened, semisweet, or milk chocolate)
1 cup heavy cream
1 Tablespoon flavor of choice: rum, cognac, espresso, or whatever meets your fancy. You can use rum flavoring, vanilla, etc. If you use the flavorings, adjust it to taste, a Tablespoon may be too strong.
Powdered sugar (see directions below for amount)

### *Directions*

That's it, 4 simple ingredients. Now you simply make a ganache: cream and chocolate. Break the chocolate into chunks and put in processor. Pulse until it is broken into small pieces or you can coarsely chop it with a knife. Place in a bowl.

Scald the cup of cream over medium-low heat until starts to boil, stirring so it doesn't scorch. Pour over chocolate and let it set a minute, then stir in flavoring and stir until smooth. Now, taste it. If the ganache is not sweet, enough for your taste, depending on what type of chocolate you used, put in ¼ cup powdered sugar and stir well. Repeat until you're happy with the taste. Remember, these are chocolate lover truffles, the dark bitterness is delightful to true chocoholics…but do them how you like them.

Chill in refrigerator for 3-4 hours or overnight. Use melon baller or measuring spoon to scoop mixture and roll into a ball. Roll in coating of your choice: ground pistachios, walnuts, pecans, cocoa powder, or nothing. Place on aluminum foil or parchment paper-lined cookie sheet. Chill and then put in covered plastic container to store. I like to put them in paper candy cups, available at Hobby Lobby and other stores, to serve them. They are very festive at Holiday time or at any time of the year. Deanna likes to spread the truffle mixture in a pan like fudge, chill, and then cut into squares before dipping in optional coatings. That works well, too. Either way, you may never make marshmallow fudge again after eating these delicious truffles!

# *GRANNIE'S COBBLER*

I've probably mentioned I grew up with lots of desserts. And with a dad and grandparents from Texas, many of those desserts were pies and cobblers. I can still see my Grannie's cobbler, blackberries oozing out of that delicate lattice crust. We never minded picking those wild blackberries when we knew a pie, cobbler, or even homemade ice cream was in store. Any fruit works with this, peaches, cherries, apricots, and apples are all favorites. Top it with a scoop of vanilla ice cream and you may think you've gone to heaven.

There are many forms of cobbler; I am sharing the kind I grew up with, fruit and a decadent crust. This isn't a biscuit dough or a batter, but is instead a richer pie-type crust. This cobbler is a rectangular or square pie with no bottom crust and a delicate top crust. Fresh fruit is always best, though frozen and canned are acceptable. I've never seen anyone turn down a piece of this cobbler. Just place the desired fruit sprinkled with sugar and cinnamon or whatever flavorings you like and add the crust.

This recipe makes enough to top two 13 x 9-inch cobblers. I usually take half of the dough, wrap it in plastic wrap, and freeze for another time. Just let the ball thaw in the fridge before using.

—Dea

## *Ingredients*

4 cups of flour
1 teaspoon salt
2 cups of shortening
1 egg, beaten
1 Tablespoon of apple cider vinegar
½ cup cold water

## *Directions*

Place flour and salt into a large bowl, mix with a fork. Cut in shortening, don't cut in as fine as for piecrust, and leave it somewhat rough. In a small bowl, beat 1 egg, add apple cider vinegar and cold water, stir to mix. Sprinkle the liquid mixture over the dough, tossing with a fork until lightly mixed. Gather dough up and divide in half, gently shape into 2 balls. Chill 15 minutes. Roll out on a floured surface to the desired size, this crust should be a little thicker than you would roll a pie crust. Leave whole or cut into strips for a lattice top, lift with a small spatula or flat knife. Don't worry if it tears, cobblers are supposed to be rustic. Place over the desired fruit filling, seal edges and sprinkle top with sugar.
Bake at 400 degrees 'til crust begins to become golden brown, usually around an hour.

## SWEETHEART COOKIES

These cookies are a sweet treat, perfect for almost any holiday or celebration. We often celebrate holidays at the ranch, including Valentine's Day, knowing we will likely have a better meal at home than in a restaurant. These make a lovely Valentine dessert with their pink color, especially if served on a pretty plate. They are equally fitting for Easter, Christmas, or a birthday party. Maraschino cherries give them the pretty color and the addition of dark chocolate and slivered almonds helps to balance the sweetness. They are unusual in that no leavening or egg is used. This will make around 2 to 2½ dozen cookies, depending on size of cookie.

—Dea

**Ingredients**

1 cup of butter
1 teaspoon of almond extract

½ teaspoon salt
1 cup of powdered sugar
2¼ cup of all-purpose flour
3 Tablespoon of maraschino juice or syrup
½ cup chopped maraschino cherries
½ cup slivered almonds
1 cup of dark chocolate morsels or chopped chunks

## Directions

Line cookie sheets with parchment paper and preheat oven to 350 degrees.

Using either a stand mixer or hand-held one, beat butter 'til creamy, add almond extract, then beat in salt, and powdered sugar. Alternate adding at low speed: flour and maraschino juice or syrup. Stir in almonds and dark chocolate morsels or chopped chunks. Roll into golf ball size or smaller balls and place on parchment-covered sheet.

Bake at 350 degrees for 12 to 18 minutes, until a few cookie edges barely show any golden color. Let stand on sheet for a few minutes before removing.

Serve on a pretty plate fitting the occasion, store leftover cookies in a cookie jar or other air-tight type container.

## *NO BAKE SOUR CREAM AND FRUIT PIE*

Summertime is the time for cool, fruity desserts. Picture this delicious pie garnished with sliced strawberries and fresh blueberries and you have the perfect 4th of July dessert. Quick, Easy, Delicious, and Beautiful! The fireworks will fly, but remember, you don't have to wait for the 4th of July. Every day is a special occasion.

—Gay G

### *Graham Cracker Crust*

### *Ingredients*

22 graham cracker squares
¼ cup sugar
¼ teaspoon salt
5 Tablespoon butter melted

### *Directions*

Crush graham crackers by placing in a large plastic food-safe bag. Use a rolling pin to break up into small pieces then roll to crush into crumbs. You can also crush them fine in a food processor.
Melt butter in a small pan; add salt and sugar. Stir to combine and pour over cracker crumbs in a medium-size bowl. Mix well until even consistency and all crumbs are "wet." Place mixture in pie pan and press to cover bottom and sides of the pan. Bake at 350 degrees for 10 minutes. Remove and cool before filling.

### *Filling*

### *Ingredients*

3 Tablespoon corn starch
1 cup milk (try buttermilk if you have extra hanging around in the refrigerator)
⅔ cup light corn syrup (or try agave syrup)
1 teaspoon clear vanilla (I have started using clear vanilla exclusively for the flavor and avoid the dark color of regular.)
1 cup sour cream (8 ounce)
1½ cup fresh blueberries or chopped ripe peeled peaches
1 Graham Cracker pie crust Readymade or homemade, your family will not care if you bought the crust, they'll just be glad you made them pie.

## *Directions*

Combine all filling ingredients except blueberries in a mixing bowl. Use an electric mixer or food processor and mix on low until all ingredients are well combined. Add blueberries and fold in gently with rubber spoon or spatula. Pour into cooled graham cracker crust. Chill in refrigerator for several hours before serving.

God Bless America and Mom's sweet desserts!

## GRANDMA'S BEST SUGAR COOKIES

John and I have a German friend who says these cookies remind him of cookies he ate as a child in Europe. A connoisseur of fine food and wine, it's fun to cook for him and we enjoy his company immensely, though he claims to "not understand this American cowboy culture at all." We'll forgive him, because he's a good pilot and a good friend.

There are a million Sugar Cookie recipes out there, but this one is exceptional. I am not a big fan of baking cookies, probably because I always get distracted and burn that last batch, but these are worth taking the time to make and bake. Enjoy!

—Gay G

## *Ingredients*

1½ cup powdered sugar
1 egg
1 cup butter
1 teaspoon vanilla
½ teaspoon almond extract
1 teaspoon cream of tartar
2½ cups flour
½ teaspoon baking soda
⅛ teaspoon salt

## *Directions*

Cream together butter & sugar until smooth, add egg, vanilla, and almond extract, and mix well. Add dry ingredients and mix until well blended. Using hands make the dough into a ball and then roll into a log. Cover in plastic wrap and chill for 3 hrs. minimum. When ready to bake simply unwrap roll, slice into ⅜ inch pieces and bake at 375 degrees for 10-12 minutes or until edges just start to brown. Experiment with the time to get cookies how you like them best. Thicker cookies will be a little softer. Frost and decorate.
Note: You can roll out the dough and cut with cookie cutter shape of choice. However, using extra flour to get the dough rolled changes the texture of cookie so you might want to experiment. The roll and cut method is easier, faster, and once decorated are delightful cookies.

## *Frosting*

¼ cup butter (½ stick)
1 teaspoon clear vanilla
1-pound box powdered sugar
2-3 Tablespoon milk (add more for thinner frosting)

Mix ingredients until smooth. This is a great frosting to use for decorating cookies. Use food color gel for vibrant colors (available at Hobby Lobby, online, and specialty stores), but liquid food coloring will also work. If you frost cookies when slightly still warm, the frosting will melt a little and then be glossy when it hardens.

## *OLD-FASHIONED SUGAR COOKIES*

This is based on an old-fashioned recipe and makes a lot of cookies, enough for a crew of hungry cowboys, a family reunion, or a kids' party. You can cut the recipe in half, if you need to. The cookies are simply delicious, with a fine cake-like crumb and are decadent with a rich icing. They are a large, soft sugar cookie, best made in a large round shape. These cookies are usually cut with a 3 to 4" cutter; you can use a gallon jar lid, a wide mouth canning jar lid, etc. A great choice for bake sales and for holidays, even birthdays. I tint the icing according to the holiday or season, pink icing for Easter, white icing for Christmas with green and red colored sugars, etc. My kids loved to also decorate them for Valentine's Day by putting a few cinnamon candies on the white buttercream icing for a great contrast in flavor.

An electric beater can be used, but don't over mix the dough. I prefer to mix this recipe by hand, though it is a pretty good work out. I think it makes a nicer texture. You can make your own colored sugar by placing a couple of Tablespoons of sugar in a small dish and adding either liquid or gel food color a drop at a time and mixing well. The actual frosting is easier using a mixer, but can also be done by hand if you want the true old-fashioned feel.

—Dea

In a small bowl mix together:
4 cups flour
2 teaspoon baking powder
2 teaspoon salt
Set aside

In a large bowl, mix together well:
1 cup shortening
½ cup butter
2 cups sugar
3 or 4 eggs
2 teaspoon flavoring, either lemon or vanilla

Gradually stir in the dry mixture. Add up to one more cup flour mixing well until you can just handle the dough. You want a soft, barely able to handle dough when done.
Chill the dough while the oven preheats to 350 degrees
Roll dough out about ¼ to ½ inch thick and cut with a large round cookie cutter or drinking glass. Don't roll too thin, these cookies are somewhat cake-like.
Place on a greased cookie sheet, do not crowd, as they will spread slightly and rise while baking
Bake until edges are just barely brown, 10 to 15 minutes, don't overbake.
Remove from the sheet after a couple of minutes and frost when cool.

## Icing

In a bowl place
½ cup shortening
½ cup butter
Or use all shortening if pure white icing is desired
Gradually add up to 4 cups of powdered sugar
Stir in 1 teaspoon flavoring and 2 teaspoon milk

You will want to drop a large dollop of icing on the cookie and spread it, not quite to the edge. The icing should be thick on the cookie, making a great luscious bite. Decorate with candies, etc. if desired.

# HINTS AND TIPS

I've learned some helpful tips over the years, some come from friends, and some I've discovered myself. I've shared some here, some are simple and pretty common, and some may have you wondering why you didn't think of doing that before, like I do. If you're like me, the hardest part is remembering to actually use them. But once you tried them and find they work for you, you're much more likely to remember and use them. Everyone loves a simple time or work saver.

When boiling pasta, boil twice the amount the recipe calls for. Take half and submerge it quickly into cold water to stop cooking. Then drain and freeze. This works really well for dishes like mac and cheese, pasta salads, and casseroles. I love having it on-hand when I suddenly need to make a side dish in a hurry. Just place the frozen bag of pasta and run it under cold water to thaw for cold dishes and under hot water for hot dishes.

Another thing I double up on is cooking bacon. Cooking bacon is always a mess, so I prefer to do it as little as possible. I often will fry it in a Dutch oven to help with splattering or place it on cookie sheets and bake it in the oven.
This tip of doubling up also works great for those few slices lurking in the fridge that need to be used. After cooking the bacon, allow it to cool a few minutes, then crumble and place in bags or small containers to place in the freezer. It is great to have on hand for recipes or for topping foods.

I also will roast extra peppers, either green chiles or other varieties. My family loves the little, colorful sweet peppers that are so pretty and great in salads or for snacking. I discovered they roast quite well and add a great note of flavor to dips and soups, etc. I either roast over a burner in the house or on the grill outside. I then chop and freeze what I don't need for later.

Since I only have my husband and myself at home now, I end up with large amounts of recipes, like stuffed peppers, smothered burritos, breakfast burritos, or lasagna, as examples. Instead of going through all the work to make just a couple of them for the two of us, I make the full recipe. I then freeze the other portions; this is our version of "convenience food" or TV dinners when you live so far out.

Like so many others, we are trying to watch our carb intake. One way I do this without totally giving up some of our favorite flavors and dishes is to replace the pasta or rice with zucchini or similar squash, or cauliflower, etc. I don't have the spiral noodle maker but have devised other ways to use the veggies. I use a mandolin to slice zucchini super thin, then salt it, and roast it to use for lasagna noodles or even tortillas in casseroles. Cauliflower can be used raw, and chopped fine or run in a food processor to replace rice in a recipe that requires the rice be cooked in the dish. The flavors in these dishes are not dependent on the pasta or rice, so you'll still get the flavors you love.

One trick I learned a long time ago is great for the less experienced cook or one who doesn't have a ton of kitchen aids. I hated trying to measure things like shortening, soft butter, or peanut butter and it makes a big mess in the measuring cup. Here's what to do, I'll give you an example. Say a recipe calls for ⅓ cup of shortening. Fill the cup with ⅔ cup of water. Add the shortening 'til the contents of the cup raise to the 1 cup level. Pour the water off and you have the right amount without smooshing and scraping.

You'll find recipes in here that utilize leftover meats and cheeses, two of the more expensive grocery items. The Bolognese recipe makes a wonderful, rich sauce that you'll make time and again, and it makes enough that you'll probably be able to freeze some. Thaw some of that frozen pasta out and you'll have a quick, delicious meal when you come in and are tired. The cheese dips recipes are great for using those cheeses that may need to be scraped and cleaned but are still useable.

I hope this helps you and might make things a bit easier in the kitchen, keep on cooking and trying new things.

—Dea

## *TUNAS / PRICKLY PEAR FRUITS*

Prickly pear fruits are often called tunas in the Southwest. They are the big, delicious fruit of the prickly pear cactus. The darker the color, the juicier, and more flavorful they will be. These ruby red fruits are easiest picked by tongs. There are all kinds of recipes for them, everything from juices, jellies, and syrups to pastry fillings. My great-grandmother from south Texas would make delicious fried pies or turnovers with a beautiful red filling. We'll just cover the basics here for folks who are new to this delicacy. I really encourage you to try this fruit; it is even available in specialty markets and grocery stores nowadays.

Tunas are ripe when they are dark red in color; I sometimes wait until some have begun to fall off the plants and split open. The paler pink stage just isn't as good. It is worth it to wait 'til they're fully ripe. No matter how tempting they look, don't pick them with your hands. They are covered with sharp, tiny stickers that need to be burned off. I suggest wearing heavy gloves; you may be like me and forget you are dealing with a food that has invisible stickers. Use tongs to twist and pull the fruit off and place it in a bucket. Because they yield a lot of juice, you don't need to pick a huge amount of them. I'd suggest you picture your Dutch oven and figure how many it would take to cover the bottom 2 fruit deep for your first batch of juice. Once you've picked them you need to deal with the tiny stickers that cover the fruits. Some folks may place them on a grill to burn the stickers off. I prefer to spread them out on a sidewalk or other non-flammable, hard surface, and use a propane-powered weed burner to burn the stickers off. You can see the tiny stickers catch fire and burn away. Just roll them over a few times to get all the stickers off. I know some folks will say they cook the tunas with the stickers still on and then strain the juice, thinking they are straining the stickers. In good conscience, I must say I've tried that and found the stickers remained, giving everyone a few stickers in their tongue and mouth. That's not pleasant.

Once you've taken care of the stickers place the fruit in your pot and cover with water. Bring to a boil, lower to a simmer and occasionally mash the fruit and stir the liquid. The fruit will split open, making a beautiful colored liquid. When they are fully split open and have begun to appear mushy, strain the liquid through a cheesecloth. You now have a lovely juice you can make jelly or syrup out of, or even cook down further with a thickener like cornstarch for a filling. I usually add 3/4 to 1 cup of sugar per cup of juice along with 1 Tablespoon of orange, lime, or lemon juice per cup for jelly or syrup. The citrus adds a nice, bright note to the juice. After adding this, you can cook the juice down more to make a syrup, cooking until you've reached the thickness you want. I use the syrup in drinks, including iced tea and lemonade, besides over ice cream, cakes, and pancakes. The taste is unique and jellies and syrups make a nice gift, too.

—Dea

# *I BURNED THE SPAGHETTI SAUCE!*

One of the motives behind writing this book was to share our love of cooking and to inspire people to cook more. However, it's not just about cooking. Anyone can learn to cook. It's about cooking and gathering people together to enjoy the food you've prepared for them. Food bonds people by bringing them together to share a common experience. Often, it reinforces our culture in a family or shares our culture with friends, acquaintances, or business people that we invite to eat with us. Sitting around a table sharing and celebrating food is a good way to get to know people and that includes your own family.

When we are together for a dinner at home, out to lunch, or dining out to celebrate a great dinner, our friend Mike Huber always makes a toast, "Here's to friends and family and friends who are like family". I love that. It always brings a smile to everyone's face. It's a beautiful sentiment. It embodies what we're about and what we want to share with you. Whether you're cooking for two or a crew, eating together brings a sense of unity to the people who are there. It provides a venue to talk to each other; it builds memories. When we wonder why there is so much sadness in our young people, so much anger, and depression, we often don't have to look farther than the dinner table. Too often there isn't one. It's a flat piece of furniture with a pile of papers and junk on it. That's a sad scene because one of the most important tools we have to bring people together is the dining room table.

Let's be part of a revolution, let's get people cooking, families and friends sitting down to eat together again. In our houses, that's the norm and the younger generations, children and grandchildren, nieces, nephews, brothers, sisters, etc., etc. love it. It keeps us all coming home, gathering together, and we are blessed. Life isn't always easy, and we've seen our share of troubles, but dinner on the table is a constant. It's consistent, predictable, reliable, and dependable. If all else fails, we can count on dinner and that is healing and comforting.

So many people don't cook these days, preferring to grab something fast or dine out at restaurants. We all do it; no one is pointing fingers. There are many reasons to skip cooking at home: convenience, too tired from a busy workday, and just plain don't want to cook or don't know how to cook. If you're lucky like I was, you grew up in a family where everyone was a fabulous cook. If you wanted fried chicken with mashed potatoes and gravy, no problem! Want homemade polenta with pheasant gravy, no problem! Want Fettucine Alfredo and Lobster, you got it! How about that Ribeye steak with baked potatoes and fresh green beans? Delish! I grew up eating fabulous food and it made me love food and want to know how to make it. If you weren't so lucky, you may not have developed an appreciation for cooking, but that doesn't have to stop you. Anyone can learn to cook; you just have to want to learn. If you look at the value, you get a good bang for your buck. Kids come home, families bond, communication opens up, and you save money. All those reasons seem to say it's worth some effort to make it happen.

If you don't cook at all right now, then start with something simple like Saturday morning pancakes for breakfast and you'll be a hero/heroine. Take some cooking classes; they're great fun for singles, couples, or friends' groups. Try a cooking school for a vacation. I once spent ten days at the cooking school at Villa Delia in Tuscany, Italy, cooking with Umberto Menghi. It was one of the most memorable vacations I have ever had!

If you're an experienced cook, get fired up and learn to be a better cook. Deanna and I are students, we are always trying to learn something new, make something better, and create a new recipe. It's great fun! For experienced cooks, I recommend the book *Salt, Fat, Acid, Heat* by Samin Nasrit. My daughter, Allison, bought the book for me and brought it when she came to visit recently. What a wonderful gift! I couldn't put it down.

Samin earned her chef wings working for Alice Waters at the famed Chez Panisse restaurant in Berkeley, California. Every home "chef" will learn something new and wonderful from her book. After all these years of cooking, I learned how to use salt correctly and it has made an amazing difference in the dishes I make. Cooking is fun and rewarding and there is always something new to learn!

Sometimes we don't cook because we're afraid of failure. "I'm just not going to go to all that work to make something that isn't good." Sound familiar? Oh, friend, we have all had failures. No one rides a two-wheel bike without falling at least once and no one that's ever cooked hasn't had cookies burn, a cake fall, or cooked a chicken that was dry and tasteless. You know what they say, "if you get bucked off, get back on." Cooking isn't much different than getting bucked off. It's a science, an art, and a learned skill. Like good horsemanship, it's a lifelong process of learning to be better. No one was born cooking, but everyone can learn to cook. No one was born riding a horse either, unless it was Doug Williamson (one of the world's best horsemen), but everyone can learn to ride a horse. We will all have a cake fall from time to time, but that's when you Cowboy-Up/Cowgirl-Up and make a Trifle!

Recently I burned the spaghetti sauce. Yep, burned it good! I've even included a picture of the pot to prove it. The irony is that I was working on this cookbook when I suddenly realized I smelled something burning. I hurried to the kitchen to turn off the stove. When the lid came off, there was the sauce cooked down to almost a paste with a hard-burned crust in the bottom of the pan. All the moisture from the beef stock and wine had steamed off. The heat was turned on low, but not on a small enough burner and I was using a Dutch oven, which conveys heat very well. That's why we like those pots, remember?

Two things were going through my mind: I don't want to start over, and I have my taste buds set on pasta and meatballs for dinner. What to do now? Deanna and I had just been talking about how we couldn't think of a time when something wasn't turning out very good that we hadn't been able to "fix it." Well, I had just created such a fixing opportunity for myself. It's not what I

had planned, but it's what my circumstances presented. I turned off the stove and grabbed another pot. Carefully, being sure not to scrape any of the burned crust off the bottom, I spooned the spaghetti sauce into the new pan. Since it was pretty thick and pasty, I poured a good portion of wine into it, gave a good stir, and put a lid on it…small burner…low heat. Later I made the meatballs, browned them in some olive oil so they would hold their shape, and then slid them into the sauce to finish cooking.

When John got home, dinner was ready. I put the meatballs in a bowl, topped them with grated Parmesan cheese, poured two glasses of wine and we sat down to eat. A few bites in, he said, "This sauce is delicious. Exceptionally good this time! Can you duplicate this sauce to put over-stuffed cabbage rolls? I think it would be great on cabbage rolls."

"Yep, I can," says I.

The next morning, he saw me giving elbow grease to the pot where I'd burned the sauce and of course asked me about it. Confession time with a smile. I find life so much richer when we can laugh at our own mistakes.

Time, age, and the wisdom and experience that comes with them turned this potential disaster into a no-big-deal event. No angst or panic. Being a good cook is easy, fun, creative, and rewarding, and it's a skill we can all develop by starting with simple things and then practicing. Soon you won't be grabbing for a recipe book every time you go into the kitchen. You'll cook with instinct and confidence and that's when the real fun begins! You'll go to a restaurant, experience a new wonderful dish, then come home and make it just as good or better for a fraction of the cost.

That brings up another reason people have said they eat out instead of cooking at home; it costs less to eat out. Since 48-50% of the money Americans spend on food is spent eating outside the home, it appears a lot of people think it's cheaper than buying the groceries and making the dinner. We're here to prove to you that is not true. In a popular food documentary, a family is shown going through a fast-food drive-through to buy dinner because the mother claims she cannot afford to buy fresh food and fix it at home. So, their dinner consists of hamburgers, French fries, and sodas. For a family of four, this meal would average $5-$7 each or $20-28 per family meal. The USDA sites the average price of cooking at home is $1.50-3.00 per meal or $6.00-12.00 per family of 4. Just for fun, using those numbers for just 1 meal a day, how much could a family save over a year's time? It calculates to just under $6000 per year savings to buy good food and cook at home. That would pay for a bigger house, a grand vacation, or be a nice addition to a savings account. And even if the savings weren't that much, what about the nutrition we're feeding our families? It's pretty evident we can eat better if we eat at home.

When we sit down to dinner at our house someone often says, "This is the best restaurant in town." Your house can be everyone's favorite place to eat, too! We've shared some of our crews' favorite recipes and hope they become some of your favorites, too.

—Gay G.

## *FOOD, FRIENDS, FAMILY, and FAITH*

If I were to make an ingredient list and recipe for a great life, I'd probably list food, friends, family, and faith. Maybe not in that order, but, they are all part of my life. I'll start with the first one, food. I am continually amazed at the quality and quantity we have available in this country. While growing up in a family that has produced food for generations, I still marvel at today's grocery stores. Farming and ranching have made tremendous strides to keep us all well fed. It is sometimes easy to forget that. When I was growing up so many foods were strictly seasonal. Now, we can have watermelon at Christmas, if we want it. We have almost unlimited choices, all due to great folks growing great food and I think those people need to be given some recognition for what they do. While I grow a garden, and raise the beef and lamb we consume, it is often for convenience. I can walk outside and pick a salad; walk over to the freezer and choose what meat I want. It also allows me to have the exact variety of something I want.

I am gifted with some of the greatest people in the world to call friends. The wonderful friend who co-authored this book, Gay Gardella and her partner, John Lynch, are two of those folks. We have ridden together, worked cattle together, been there for each other in times of need, and we share a table very often. Gay's background in beef production and agricultural in general, along with John's extensive veterinarian practice and agricultural experience play a big role in our food and lifestyle. John and my husband are good buddies and manage to grill and smoke meat to perfection between discussions of cattle and horses.

Family is one of the reasons I learned to cook. My mother was not a cook or a baker. I learned because I liked the great food I got at grandparents and other family members' homes. I also learned to bake before I learned to cook. The first breakfast I served my husband after we were married was unforgettable: chili, fried eggs, and vinegar pie. That will give you an idea of how much I had to learn. When I started having kids, I wanted to feed them the best I could, like most mothers do. I love to feed our kids and grandkids and I especially love showing the kids healthier ways to cook things, while still sharing and enjoying old fashioned, family recipes.

Faith is my last ingredient. I believe everyone needs to believe in something, no matter your religion or beliefs. I believe that the Good Lord is there when we need him, that things happen for reasons beyond our understanding, and that we can and will get beyond some of life's greatest tragedies. I also believe that if you take all of these ingredients, food, family, friends and faith, blend and fold them together, you'll find it is really all you will ever need to have a great life.

—Dea

www.ingramcontent.com/pod-product-compliance
Lightning Source LLC
Chambersburg PA
CBHW060752150426
42811CB00058B/1380